HUNTING?
Don't Forget the Toilet Paper!

A Guide to Successful Hunting

To David Kirby, a long time friend
Christmas, 2000
Don Lamm Jr.
Richard E. Cooper

HUNTING?
Don't Forget the Toilet Paper!

A Guide to Successful Hunting

BY

**Don Lamm, Jr. and
Richard E. Cooper**

A division of Squire Publishers, Inc.
4500 College Blvd.
Leawood, KS 66211
1/888/888-7696

Copyright 2000
Printed in the United States

ISBN: 1-58597-051-4

Library of Congress Control No. 00 134347

LEATHERS
PUBLISHING

A division of Squire Publishers, Inc.
4500 College Blvd.
Leawood, KS 66211
1/888/888-7696

In memory of Frank "Ike" Russell, the best pheasant shot we ever saw, and who had the uncanny ability to always be in the right place at the right time.

1930-2000

CONTENTS

INTRODUCTION

THIS BOOK contains true short stories about unforgettable outdoor adventures experienced over the past 60 years by the co-authors and their friends or relatives. By far, the majority deal with quail, pheasant and turkey hunting, but some are about waterfowl and fishing. One is even about a pet crow.

Each story is filled with the most memorable moments of each hunting adventure, and the authors hope that readers will find them as enjoyable as the people who experienced them.

This is not a "how-to" book, although several of the stories contain tips and guidelines on ways to be a more successful hunter under a given set of circumstances. Basically, it's a "we did it, right or wrong" book which includes a lot of quirky experiences.

Of invaluable assistance in recalling these experiences and their dates is a hunting trip diary which Richard kept over most of a 49-year period. Relevant data recorded on the backs of photographs also helped immensely.

Since prehistoric times, humans have pursued the hunt, and this pursuit has become firmly ingrained in our culture. When people share such common experiences, a deep camaraderie is established which is scarcely exceeded by any other. This especially applies to a father and his sons and increasingly so between father and daughters and husband and wife.

Today, modern scientific game management has returned many species of birds and animals to abundance which otherwise would be nearing extinction. All the hunting experiences described in this book were made possible by this tireless conservation work on the part of state agencies with funding assistance from a federal tax on firearms and ammunition.

Tragically, there are two ominous threats to the American hunter today. First is the relentless effort to impose more so-called "gun control" laws on the general population. Many who have led this campaign over the years openly profess an objective of total firearms confiscation from all except law enforcement and military personnel. Part and parcel of their intentions is repeal of the Second Amendment of the Bill of Rights. Their efforts are based on the simplistic reasoning that removal of guns from the populace will also remove crime from the populace. The fact that an alarming number of unthinking citizens have been convinced by an hysterical news media of the validity of this idea poses the greatest single threat to American freedom today.

A disarmed populace is a populace helpless to resist tyranny. Such evil will prevail if good men (and women) do nothing!

Crime and violence will never be removed from American society. The best way to keep it in check, and hopefully reduce it, is through the teaching of responsibility to our youth, the utilization of responsibility by parents, and the rigid enforcement of existing state and local laws which are directed toward law breakers not law abiding citizens.

The second threat to the sport of hunting is the fanatical anti-hunter movement, identified by such organizations as the Fund for Animals, People for the Ethical Treatment of Animals (PETA), and similar animal rights groups. These tunnel-visioned groups' objectives would cut off the financial life blood of conservation agencies which have managed large numbers of wildlife so successfully. Organizations such as Ducks Unlimited, Quail Unlimited and the National Turkey Federation, which raise millions of additional dollars for wildlife management each year, would no longer exist since these organizations are made up entirely of hunters.

Remove hunting from the American scene, and a deer surplus beyond our wildest dreams will occur. The economies of many central and western states will suffer, and a wholesome and rewarding activity will be lost forever.

ACKNOWLEDGMENTS

The authors gratefully acknowledge the patience and support of their wives, Mae Cooper and Connie Lamm, during the preparation and publication of this book.

Both authors deeply appreciate the permission granted by Lloyd and Ella Libal, Dail and Joyce Applegate, and Mike Fallis and family of Kansas and Scott and Brenda Hoffman of Iowa for allowing them to hunt their properties since the early 1960s. These are very special people. Also, our thanks to the numerous other farmers in Missouri, Kansas and Iowa for granting us permission to hunt over the years as well. Without them, none of the hunts written about in this book would have been possible.

We are grateful to Bob Lamm for guiding us on a number of memorable quail and pheasant hunts in Iowa and Kansas, and Don is most appreciative to Bob and Art, his sons, and to his brother-in-law, Virgil Tagtmeyer, for helping him to find and call turkeys to within gun range.

Don also extends his gratitude to Rush and Inez Johnson of Bucklin, Missouri and to Don and Audrey Walsworth of Marceline, Missouri, for sponsoring his membership into Turkey Creek Farm, Inc., a waterfowl club in which he was a member and part owner for over thirty years. He experienced many a thrilling day with his friends watching and hunting ducks and geese next to the Swan Lake National Wildlife Reservation in Chariton County, Missouri.

THE AUTHORS

We are two middle-class characters who have never been affluent enough to afford as much free time as we would have liked for hunting nor to invest in the type of equipment and dogs which we would have desired most. Our hunting trips were always squeezed into weekends or holiday vacations, oftentimes much to the displeasure of family members.

However, over the years we have had many memorable experiences, some quite frankly we would like to forget. We have included some of each in this book.

The Cast of Characters
Other than the Authors

Bill Glenn — Retired banker residing in Sedalia and a friend of Don Lamm since childhood. He hunted with the authors for 30 years until forced to give up the sport in 1992 because of an arthritic hip.

Bob Lamm — Don's younger son who started hunting with his father at age 11. He is now a professional guide, serving trout fishermen in the spring and summer in eastern Idaho, pheasant hunters in the fall in southwestern Iowa, and turkey hunters in the spring in Missouri.

Art Lamm — Don's older son who grew up hunting quail with his father in Missouri and now resides in Oregon where his favorite targets are pheasants and chukars. He is known for keeping a meticulous diary of all his hunting experiences.

Jay Cooper — Richard's older son who lives in Sedalia. Although left-handed, he never lets it bother him, as his favorite gun is a conventionally built 20-gauge semi-automatic. Under parental influence, he grew up with the 20-gauge.

Eric Cooper — Richard's younger son who is somewhat of a maverick, shooting a Remington 12-gauge pump. He is a corporal in the Missouri Highway Patrol and resides in Mountain Grove, Missouri.

Mel Shearburn — Richard's father-in-law and father of his first wife, Gayle. Slight of built, Mel had a magnetic, down-home personality. After his family, his great loves were quail hunting, antique collecting and long evenings of playing pitch. He died in 1985.

Bob Edmondson — A classic example of the benefits to be gained from a rigorous physical fitness program. Although well into his 70s, he is the freshest member of the hunting party after a long day in the field. Although a retired teacher, he still works a full schedule as a crop insurance claims adjuster.

Walt Diehl — A teaching colleague and hunting companion from the early 1960s who is now retired and lives in Mexico, Missouri. It was through his encouragement that the authors decided to write this book.

Frank Russell — The luckiest hunter who ever packed a shotgun, always being in the right spot when a rooster exploded from the brush. Being a remarkably accurate shot also figured in establishing his usual role of top gun of the day. He retired in 1984 after teaching history and government at Smith-Cotton High School in Sedalia, Missouri, for 30 years. Frank died at the age of 70 as this book was being written. The authors were pallbearers at his funeral.

HOW TO MAKE A MEDIOCRE HUNT A GREAT HUNT

Richard Cooper, 1977

A GREAT PHEASANT HUNT doesn't have to include getting one's daily limit every day. A mediocre shooting performance can be turned into a great hunt with some outstanding dog work or a few moments of good shooting at the end of the hunt. Such was the case in a three-day hunt in early November of 1977 in which I was fortunate enough to participate.

Three of us had driven from Sedalia, Missouri to our favorite pheasant haunt in north-central Kansas for the season opener. All of us were teachers. Don Lamm taught at State Fair Community College in Sedalia, and Frank Russell and I at Smith-Cotton High School, which is the community's public high school. Don had taught there for six years before transferring to the junior college.

Don and I traveled in one vehicle, and Frank and his wife, Delta, in another. Delta didn't hunt, but she provided a valuable service by picking us up when we completed a walk through a field and returning some of us to our other vehicle.

Don and I had taken days of personal leave for the Monday

Frank Russell with his great Brittany, Snap, after a successful pheasant hunt in north-central Kansas, November 10, 1974.

1

after the season opened, which gave us a good two and one-half days of hunting. Frank and Delta were reluctant to do this, so this left Don and I to hunt alone on Monday.

Don and I did only fair, not because of a lack of pheasants, but because of disappointingly poor shooting. For Frank, that wasn't a problem. He was deadly with his old J. C. Higgins 12-gauge pump and consistently outshot us.

The first two days were cloudy and chilly with considerable fog. However, the third day was bright and sunny with the temperature rising to near 60 degrees. It was under those conditions that Don and I were finishing up around noon.

As we were nearing the south end of the section which we had hunted with modest success, three roosters flew from a shallow draw out over our parked truck and settled in the fenced corner of a field on the other side of the narrow dirt road. We had earlier hunted this field with no success whatever. We reigned in our dogs, put leashes on them, and crawled through the fence, hoping to trap the roosters

Don Lamm, Frank Russell and Richard Cooper (left to right), taking a break after a successful morning of pheasant hunting in Osborne County, Kansas. November 5, 1977.

The co-authors with a limit of Iowa ringnecks along an Adams County, Iowa cornfield, October 30, 1993.

in the corner. Each of us was convinced that all three had hit the ground with their landing gear going full tilt and likely would be far away long before we got to the corner. Such was not the case as they remained exactly where they had flown in. We released the dogs and almost immediately one of them went on point. A couple of steps toward the dog, and all three birds were in the air. Three shots rang out, and three roosters came tumbling down, one in the middle of the dirt road. Instantly, the previous frustrations of the two and one-half days were forgotten. A mediocre hunt had become a great hunt.

MISERY,
SOMETIMES THE PRICE OF SUCCESS

Richard Cooper, 1983

Pheasant HUNTING isn't for the weak-hearted or the tender-foot. It requires the capacity to undergo physical abuse while diligently pursuing a bird which is admittedly smarter than any one of us. Don and I have often said that success in putting John Ringneck and his kindred brethren into the game bag is dependent on the three Ps of dedicated hunting: patience, perseverance, and perspiration. Some frustrated hunters may be inclined to add a fourth P, profanity. However, if there are ladies in the hunting party, that addition should probably be put aside.

Two of the three Ps served us well on a memorable two-day hunt near Lenox, Iowa in mid-November 1983. No perspiration on that trip; it was wet and cold the first day as it snowed continually from about 11 a.m. on into the night.

We had driven to Iowa from our homes in Sedalia, Missouri, in the wee hours of the morning. We parked on a dry, minimally maintained road next to the section of land on which we intended to hunt. As the snow began to fall and continued for a few hours, I began to get concerned about where we had parked and wondered if the old road would become too muddy for my little two-wheel drive compact pickup. The temperature was just above freezing, and the snow melted as it fell.

My concern proved to be justified around mid-afternoon. We each had our limit of three roosters and headed back to the truck when our wet and cold dogs took charge of the hunt. Both sat down, refused to budge, and glared at us with expressions which seemed to say, "Enough is enough! No farther, not one more inch!" The only way they could have been moved would have been by carrying them or dragging them through the brush.

Co-authors less than two hours after great success in newly fallen snow. A warm south wind melted it quickly. West of Creston, Iowa, November 13, 1983.

Admitting to ourselves that the dogs had more sense than we did, I headed out by myself for the truck and left Don with the dogs in a ditch along the section's west side. I told him that if I was not back in 30 minutes to pick up him and the dogs, I would be stuck. My worst fears came to pass; I was mired down almost to the axles.

A muddy trek for nearly a mile up the old road to the nearest farm house resulted in much needed help. The young farmer and a friend were watching a football game on television since it was far too miserable outside to do any work. They were remarkably congenial, although they were probably wondering to themselves why this blamed fool had no better sense than to be out in such inclement weather.

To my amazement, they jumped into a compact pickup with four-wheel drive and had me onto an adjoining gravel road in no more than 15 minutes. When he was reluctant to accept any compensation for the tow, I pressed a $20 bill into his hand and felt that I had gotten out of the predicament very fortunately indeed.

When I finally picked up Don and the dogs, all were in a state of advanced suffering, probably thinking they would never see me again. However, a night at a motel in Creston and the dogs in a warm kennel in the back of my truck, and we were ready for a second day's hunt.

That turned out to be a pheasant hunter's dream. The sky was clear, and one inch of snow had accumulated overnight on the ground. Returning to a field adjacent to the one where we had taken such punishment the day before, we found the pheasants unwilling to fly unless virtually stepped on. The dogs would be frozen on point while our tramping through a small patch of brush produced nothing. Only if nudged by a boot would a bird fly, and all of them turned out to be roosters. In less than an hour we had our limit.

We located a nearby abandoned farm house where we took pictures and dressed our birds. Then we headed for home, firmly convinced that the price which we paid the preceding day in the form of extreme discomfort and $20 was well worth it.

LATE SEASON COLD, HOT SHOOTING

Richard Cooper, 1995

NEARLY ALL OF US in the broad category of sportsmen enjoy the relative comfort of early season pheasant hunting across the Central Plains. It's the time that we harvest the young and dumb roosters who have not yet learned the fine points of survival. However, late season hunting oftentimes produces even greater success for those who can withstand the abuse of wind and snow with temperatures frequently in the single digits. We are speaking of hunting throughout January in Kansas and Nebraska and as late as January 10 in Iowa.

Don, his son Bob and I hit the jackpot in snowy north-central Kansas in early January of 1995. Don and Bob had driven out from their homes in Sedalia, Missouri, while I had driven out from Lamar, Missouri, having moved there from Sedalia just two years before. Our base of operations was a motel in Russell.

Four inches of snow lay on the ground when we started the first day of a three-day hunt. A lot of grumbling was heard when we stumbled across the rough terrain of frozen milo stubble fields.

On the first day, we started in a large switch grass field in the shape of an L, hunting the outside edge of the long side of the L. We walked three abreast, separated by about 15 yards. Don was nearest the edge, I was farthest inside, and Bob was in the middle with his two black labs. Don's setter, Zip, was quartering 25 to 30 yards in front of him.

It doesn't always happen this way, but on that sweep the man on the outside edge got most of the shooting. In hardly more than 15 minutes, Don downed and picked up his limit of four roosters. I walked over toward Bob shaking my head in amazement, and he exclaimed, "Dad's on fire over there!" Indeed he was; it was a remarkable streak of shooting.

Day two also provided some satisfying shooting, but the most memorable part of that day was the near loss of Zip. Don will relate that in another part of this book.

Day three was a gamble with the elements. Weather reports after the first day's hunt mentioned a storm brewing in the southwest and possibly heading in our direction carrying significant amounts of snow. Our second day's hunt would not be affected, but it might be wise to cancel the third day and head for home. Since the storm slowed a bit, we decided to take our chances and headed for John Ringneck's stomping (crowing, maybe) grounds again.

Light snow started by mid-morning, and the wind picked up out of the southeast to at least 20 miles per hour. It soon became punishing, but we stuck to our early morning decision and bore on. No one made any admission of bad judgment, but I'm sure that each of us was silently saying to himself that we were a bunch of looneys.

One section of land proved especially productive. The northeast one-fourth of it was on a gentle slope which was really a part of the western edge of Kansas' version of a mountain range. I'm speaking of the flint hills which are dark and brooding in winter, but gorgeously beautiful with native grasses and wildflowers in spring and summer. That quarter of the section is divided by a draw which provided us with some excellent shooting, some even over points. The birds were holding tight and didn't want to go airborne into the wind and driving snow. I blamed my poor shooting on that, also too much protective clothing and poor visibility in the continuing snow.

It was a long walk into the wind to get back to Bob's Suburban. After we arrived, we slowly thawed out as a discussion ensued on the advisability of packing it in and heading for the motel and possibly for home. Final decision — head for the motel.

However, that decision was soon to be reversed as we drove around the northwestern corner of the section. Bob spied a draw sheltered by a fairly steep bank on the northern edge of the section, a draw which Don and I had hunted for years with little or no success. We discouraged the idea of hunting it, but Bob insisted that's where pheasants would be in this type of weather. I should add at this point that Bob makes a living in the fall guiding pheasant hunters in southwest Iowa and waterfowl hunters in north and central Missouri. In May through October, he guides trout fishing expeditions on the Madison, Henry's Fork of the Snake, and other rivers of

Don Lamm, Bob Lamm and Richard Cooper on the day that Don was "green with envy," January 5, 1995.

eastern Idaho. He's one of the few persons I know who has made a good living out of doing what he loves to do most. Therefore, I yielded to his experience and knowledge and agreed to accompany him to the draw. Don held to his decision not to go, saying that he was too cold and tired.

Casually, I threw a challenge at him. "All right, Don, you stay here, but I hope we both get two birds apiece and come back here and make you green with envy." Little did I know how prophetic that offhand challenge would be.

Bob and I approached the sheltered draw from the downwind end with his more experienced lab at heel. We had taken scarcely more than one or two steps into it when pheasants seemed to explode in all directions. I dropped two roosters with my first two shots, but missed an easy opportunity with the third. Bob dropped two with his Superposed, but with it there was no third chance. By the way, that is precisely the reason that I don't care for a stack barrel or side-by-side in pheasant hunting. They penalize the hunter at the precise time he needs a third shot the most. When we returned to the Suburban, grinning from ear to ear, Don already had his admission speech prepared. "I'm green with envy, guys. I'm really green with envy."

That ended the hunt on a truly high note. A stop for picture taking was followed by a punishing dressing of birds on the lee side of an abandoned rock house, the price you pay for success.

Back at the motel in Russell, we learned that a winter storm warning was in effect for the entire area. The wise thing to have done was leave ahead of the storm, but we were so tired that we decided to ride it out until the next morning. After a good night's sleep, we found that good fortune had smiled on us. Only two of the expected six inches of snow had fallen, and it was rapidly tapering off.

We dressed and headed for a nearby restaurant where all of us put away huge breakfasts. Then after packing, we said good-bye and headed for our homes in our respective vehicles down snow-packed Interstate 70. It was tricky for about 75 miles, but at Salina we encountered only wet pavement, and it became dry pavement well before Topeka.

Crazy, you say? Sure, but what a collection of priceless memories and pictures which we will have for the rest of our lives.

CHECK EVERY LIKELY SPOT

Richard Cooper, 1979

NEARLY ALL of our pheasant hunting over the years has been in small groups, two to four hunters, maybe six at the most. This requires an approach much like hunting bobwhite quail, use of a dog, preferably one which stays close, and a good knowledge of your dog so that you know when he or she is trailing game. It is a far different situation than being in a crowd of hunters who spread out ten abreast in a cut grain field and march toward several blockers at the other end.

If I were choosing a dog strictly for pheasants, I would pick a retriever which stays naturally within 20 to 25 yards of the hunter and can easily be trained to stay closer if desired. If you know your retriever, you can readily tell when it has gotten close to a bird. Don's son, Bob, has had both goldens and black labs which have been outstanding in locating ringnecks without flushing them out of range. After the bird has been brought down, there is absolutely no better dog in locating cripples or birds dropped in extremely heavy cover.

Among the pointing breeds, Brittanies and German shorthairs are good choices if they have been trained to stay close. However, I've seen some of these breeds, especially Brittanies, that hit the ground with their landing gear going full tilt and head for the nearest horizon. Leave these dogs in the kennel when going on a pheasant hunt. Some English setters do well, but many of them push birds into the air out of shotgun range. It's a rare pointer which can be counted on to hunt close. There are some of the more exotic breeds which have gotten high marks from some pheasant hunters, but I will reserve judgement on them simply because of lack of experience on my part.

These are the ideal dogs, which most of us will never have the good fortune to own. Instead, we secure a dog which serves a number of purposes, quail, pheasants, doves maybe, and in some cases even waterfowl. That's simply the breaks of life for the average guy who likes to hunt.

I refer to "guy" out of force of habit. In reality, women are getting into the sport in increasing numbers. It's great to have them share the great hunting experience with us even though it does require the men to clean up their act a bit. In fact, my late wife, Gayle, accompanied me on several of my trips in our younger years, and later I'll relate one of our memorable experiences together pursuing ringnecks in newly fallen snow.

Now, to fulfill the above title. Checking every spot is much like making that last cast to a tempting spot at the end of a day's fishing. It always holds the promise of being productive.

It was November 1979, and I had accompanied Don to southwest Iowa for my first pheasant hunt in that state. He began hunting there a few years earlier. It was a cold day with patches of ice and snow on the ground as we followed our setters along a brushy border fence between fields of corn stubble. We were just west of Lenox in Taylor County. A small clump of brush no larger than an automobile was well out in the field a good 50 yards from the fence where an outcropping of rock had prevented planting. I told Don that I would check it out and headed for it. My setter headed that direction also, but luckily I got there first. As I approached, a hiding rooster exploded into the air, and I dropped him onto the frozen ground at about 35 yards. The moral here is obvious. Leave no likely spot unvisited. It may hold your next bird.

TIMES WHEN WEATHER DIDN'T COOPERATE (OR, MAKING THE BEST OF A BAD SITUATION)

Richard Cooper, 1971-1997

As MANY TIMES as my friends and I have gone hunting over the years, we were bound to encounter incidents of unfavorable weather. Looking back over more than four decades of hunting trip diaries, several foul weather encounters stand out. Some of them are especially frustrating, and a few induce chuckles now that the feeling of frustration has mellowed over the years. Permit me to relate five of them.

Throughout much of the decade of the 1970s, Don Lamm, Bill Glenn, and I had a regular Saturday morning routine during November. Bill, who was a banker and part-time farmer, would finish his chores early on his farm northeast of Sedalia and load up his truck for the trip into town to pick up Don and me. At that time, Don and I lived only a block apart, and my house was always the last stop.

November of 1971 was a month of regular and excessive rains. The pattern was established at the beginning of the month that the weekends would be a time of absolute certainty for long periods of heavy rain. Bill and Don would arrive at my house around 8 a.m. with windshield wipers going full tilt, hopeful that the rain would subside and that we would be able to get in several hours of bird hunting after all. Sharing their misguided optimism, I would load my dogs, shotgun, and shell bag into the back of Bill's covered truck bed and then climb into the cab, sack lunch in hand, to wait out the nasty situation.

While waiting for a quick end to the rain, we would proceed to arrive at obvious solutions to many of the world's problems and wonder why such solutions hadn't been implemented months or even years ago by people who surely were wiser than we.

After a couple of hours ruminating amongst ourselves with the rain continuing to fall, it became apparent that the day's hunt was literally a washout. By this time, our lunch sacks had been frequently visited, and our midday snacks had been largely consumed by midmorning.

On one of those miserable Saturdays the rain ended by noon, and we got in a half-day's hunt. However, the vegetation was wet, and the ground was sloppy making it an exercise in misery and frustration. Still, it was just something which dedicated quail hunters had to do.

December was only slightly better. Unseasonably mild temperatures dictated that precipitation continue to be in the form of rain rather than snow, and on some weekends we continued to hunt in a steady drizzle. We might have surrendered to the near continual abuse of the elements had it not been that 1971 saw quail numbers in Missouri at an extremely high level.

Rain also was an unwelcome visitor on a pheasant hunting trip which Frank Russell and I made to north-central Kansas in early November of 1974.

We had driven out from our homes in Sedalia in my little Datsun pickup during the late afternoon and evening before the November 9th season opener. We put up at Art Riley's Lazy L Motel in Osborne having made our reservations several months in advance. Although we did not encounter a drop of rain during the entire eight-hour trip, the mention of rain in the forecast was still upsetting.

It became far more upsetting when we awoke early the next morning to a steady patter on the roof. The drive to our chosen hunting site was through a continual moderate rain; our worst fears had come to pass.

The mud was heavy and sticky as we struggled down the last leg of the drive to our final destination. The closer we got, the worse the driving surface became. From a paved federal highway, we turned onto a sloppy but very negotiable macadamized county road. From it, we entered a lesser maintained road and slithered on for a final mile. Mud and snow tires on my little Datsun helped, but I began to wonder if we weren't about to encounter conditions which even they could not handle.

When we waddled to a final stop, we had gotten off of the driving surface as far as we dared. Thinking ahead, I began to have doubts about us ever getting back to the security of the paved federal high-way. All the while, the rain continued to fall.

After sitting in the cab for nearly an hour, the rain seemed to slacken, but it had by no means ceased. I finally observed to Frank that very few pheasants were ever shot inside the cab of a truck, and therefore I was going to brave the rain and mud and head out for some deep draws in the middle of the field we intended to hunt. He agreed with my premise but chose to hunt some closer draws in the field across the road since we had permission to hunt on both properties.

We broke out our shotguns after uncaging our dogs and headed out. At this point, I made a bad blunder. Instinctively, I locked the truck since we had valuable items inside and pocketed the key, failing to realize that Frank would be locked out if he returned first. The thought never occurred to him either so he had to share at least part of the blame for what happened.

My walk to two draws was one featuring the worst of things overhead and underfoot, a continual light rain and an utter sea of mud. However, the long walk under the most difficult of circumstances paid off. I harvested a rooster from each draw, and my diligent but soaked setter retrieved both.

When I returned to the truck, Frank was nowhere in sight so I unlocked the camper cover and returned my dog to his dry cage. The noise alerted Frank and his Brittany who had sought refuge from the continuing cold rain under a nearby wooden bridge since the truck was locked. As they approached, I could see Frank shivering from the cold. Not until we got the cab warm did he finally get over the shakes and begin a conversation which was anything more than a few agonized phrases. We could eventually chuckle over it, but it was far more of a blunder on my part than his. Even after warming up in the cab, we still weren't out of our difficulties. The continuing rain had made the road and its shoulder a sodden mess, and we were thoroughly stuck. Fortunately, I carried strap-on chains with me and put them on while getting nearly as chilled as Frank. He offered to push as I revved the engine, and finally the little pickup began to move. For fear of getting stalled again, I continued to spin and struggle forward for about 500 yards up a gradual slope to where the road became level and a gravel surface began. At that point, I stopped and removed the chains while waiting for my still wet and exhausted companion to catch up.

The rain ended shortly afterward, but our desire for any more hunting that day had largely been extinguished. Two hunters, their clothing, and the floor of my truck cab were badly in need of a thorough cleanup when we returned to the motel. Art came by as we exited the truck and showed only the slightest trace of a smile as he said, "Been kind of a tough day out there, hasn't it?" Amen!

Inclement weather produced a much more potentially dangerous situation as Don Lamm, Bob Edmondson and I were heading out for the Kansas ringneck opener in 1995.

As we drove west from Kansas City on Interstate 70, we encountered occasional light rain along with a few snow flurries, neither of which were in the forecast. The pavement was still fairly dry as the precipitation was light and sporadic. However, as we approached Junction City, it began to increase noticeably which gave us pause to wonder what we were getting into. When we made two stops there, one to refuel our thirsty Suburban and the other to refuel ourselves, we discovered a growing layer of ice on the surface making walking a tricky undertaking.

As we left the restaurant, Bob observed that unless things improved, we would be proceeding at a considerably reduced speed for the rest of the trip. Don and I appreciated Bob's caution, especially since he was driving. We proceeded at speeds of no more than 35 to 40 miles per hour, and everything seemed to go well even though the pavement was still very wet.

Suddenly, Bob let out a whoop and exclaimed, "Here we go!" Immediately, we could feel the rear of the fully loaded vehicle move counterclockwise as all control was lost, and after a spin of 180 degrees, we slid into the center median rear end first. Fortunately, no one was close behind us, and the median was relatively solid. When a break in the traffic occurred, Bob shifted into four-wheel drive, and we easily climbed back onto the driving surface again.

We pussyfooted a few more miles and suddenly drove out of the rain and onto dry pavement. The rest of the trip was filled with sighs of relief from our narrow brush with disaster and an occasional remark about the need to change our underwear. Another example of the need for toilet paper on a hunt!

The huge snowstorm that buried north-central Kansas, southeast Nebraska and southwest Iowa in October 1997, could not accurately be called a blizzard since it did not have the qualifying characteristics of strong winds and sub-freezing temperatures. However, it was sufficient to strand thousands of motorists including the three pheasant hunters noted in the preceding story.

We had hunted in a light rain all day on Saturday, the 25th, which was opening day in Iowa. When we returned to our motel room in Creston that night, we learned that a winter storm warning had been issued, a warning which we didn't take very seriously. After all, the temperature was still well above freezing, and it was still October.

Early the next morning, I was first to get both feet on the floor and peeked out through the drapes on the front window of our room. Good grief! Our Suburban was a huge white mound, and the snow was still falling heavily. I pulled on some clothing and my boots and stepped out to check the thermometer which I always hang outside before going to bed while on a hunting trip. It read 37 degrees which was proof positive that it could snow a heck of a lot faster than the comparatively warm air could melt it. My meteorological trip outside also revealed a snow depth of five inches.

We cranked up the coffeepot and broke out our breakfast bars for our usual in-house breakfast before we made a decision on how to cope with the winterish turn of events. We eventually decided to load everything as though we were heading home, but if the roads were not too bad, we would spend a few hours hunting John Ringneck in the snow.

We followed U.S. 34 to the east edge of town to where we would normally turn onto a side road that led to our favorite pheasant haunt. Long before we got to the road, our decision had been made. The highway was barely traversable, and the side road, which did not have even so much as one set of tracks on it, would have been impossible.

With the rest of the hunt abandoned, we headed east toward Osceola and what we hoped would be much better conditions on Interstate 35. It was a tense, fishtailing trip of 28 miles that required virtually an hour, and the snow seemed to get deeper the closer we got to Osceola.

The heavy wet snow clung to trees and power lines and plastered over all highway traffic signs. That, plus my boneheaded misinterpretation as to the entrance ramp to the interstate, put us onto the parking lot of a farm machinery equipment dealer. Good old four wheel drive bailed us out of the embarrassing situation, and soon

Bob capably had us on the interstate and headed for home.

Our spirits were buoyed for only about two miles when the snowfall became so heavy that visibility dropped to zero. Bob eased the Suburban to a near stop, but somehow or other by the time it stopped moving, we were off the pavement and into the center median, a rather familiar predicament considering our adventure near Junction City, Kansas just two years before.

Four wheel drive could not come to the rescue this time so we bailed out and caught a ride back into Osceola with a kind and understanding snowplow operator. We spent five hours at a truck stop just off the interstate in Osceola before a towing service could finally work us into its busy schedule. While there, we learned that the snow was indeed heavier in Osceola than in Creston. The depth at Osceola varied between 12 and 15 inches! The five hours at the truck stop were not entirely wasted. We had an experience which did wonders in broadening our vocabularies in an area where we must have been lacking. We were in an upstairs lounge room for truckers when a lady (?) trucker engaged someone in a telephone conversation discussing a third party whom she obviously disliked. Her vocabulary of profanities was something to behold. It even surpassed in variety and inventiveness the passages which Shakespeare wrote into *Hamlet*. There were many magnificently crafted phrases which I had never even considered the possibility of before.

Anyway, after we finally had our vehicle pulled from its snowy resting place, we headed south for home on a rapidly thawing interstate. By the time we reached the Missouri border, we had driven entirely out of the early season storm's path.

It turned out to be a genuine learning experience. Never underestimate how severe a winter storm can be, even in October; and, wow, what a vocabulary!

Wisdom must surely grow with increasing age. At least that seems to be an obvious conclusion when looking back on a Saturday morning hunt in early December which Don Lamm, Bill Glenn, and I had in the middle 1960s.

It was cold (middle 20s) and a light snow was falling. However, since it was a Saturday and the quail season was still open, everything dictated that we head out in pursuit of the highly esteemed bobwhite.

We headed east from Sedalia to hunt on some land owned by

Don's cousin, Beasmore. The snow had begun to pick up in intensity by the time we parked at a gate leading into the field we were going to hunt.

After we had fruitlessly walked for nearly an hour, the snow was falling even more heavily and beginning to accumulate under foot. A northeast wind had increased in velocity, and the temperature was undoubtedly a few degrees lower than when we had started.

Bill then chose that point to quote a statement his wife had made earlier in the morning as he left the house. "My wife says that all three of us are crazy."

By then, all three dogs were running about 50 yards ahead of us and stopping to walk in a tight circle in preparation to bed down. They had had it for the day.

We finally resigned ourselves to defeat and walked back to the truck through the swirling snow. We stored our shotguns and loaded three very cold setters who, along with Bill's wife, were much wiser than we.

Don Lamm, Bill Glenn and Richard Cooper (left to right) relax for a lunch break after a morning of success near Diagonal, Iowa, November 5, 1983.

Not all the birds were theirs, but Walt Diehl and Bob Edmondson are proud of their portion of the day's take in central Kansas, November 13, 1999.

IT'S A GALS' SPORT, TOO

Richard Cooper, 1960

AFTER GRADUATING from Kansas State University in 1959, Gayle and I moved to Wichita where I took a job in production at KARD-TV, which would later become the flagship station for the Kansas State Network. The location was close enough to the pheasant range in Kansas to allow travel to and from some choice spots in the north-central part of the state while still getting in a half day's hunt. This afforded me my first opportunity to hunt the ringneck pheasant.

Richard, father-in-law Mel Shearburn, and wife Gayle after a goose hunt at Turkey Creek Farm in Chariton County, Missouri, October 28, 1979.

21

Gayle and I had been married just two years, and she was quite willing to venture out into the draws and brushy fields with me. The only problem was that we didn't have a dog. This hampered us, and a number of crippled birds were lost as a result. Nevertheless, we ventured forth, equipped with quality shotguns which we were now able to afford since both of us were working. She carried a Remington Model 58 in 20-gauge, and I a Browning Light 12. Those were the days when I thought the largest cannon with the most powerful shell was necessary to be successful on ringnecks. Later, I learned differently, and in the years to follow I killed far more birds with her Remington 20-gauge, eventually shelving the Browning altogether.

It was in November, 1960, that three of my co-workers and I had a short and only moderately successful hunt in Osborne County. Rain moved in, so we headed back to Wichita. The following Saturday morning at a terribly early hour, Gayle and I headed north up U.S. 81 to try the same area again.

As we passed through Salina, we began to see signs of patchy snow on the ground, and the farther we drove the deeper it got. When we arrived at our Osborne County destination, there were at least five inches on the ground, and parking our old '54 Chevy became rather tricky. We bailed out at a farm where I had secured permission to hunt the year before and headed for a huge draw which wound northward for nearly a mile. In fact, 40 years later I still hunt the same draw with permission granted by the next generation of owner.

In less than an hour, we would have a heart-stopping experience in pheasant hunting which would be etched in our memories for the rest of our lives. Walking on opposite sides of the draw, we approached a point where it made a rather sudden 90-degree turn to the right. Before we got to the turn, I encountered pheasant tracks in the newly fallen snow so numerous that a clearly defined track was almost impossible to find. I signaled to Gayle that there were birds ahead, and she slowly approached the bend in the draw. When I got to the turn on my side, I peered over a patch of short wild plum trees and was greeted by an explosion of wings and squawking roosters, the likes of which I have never experienced since. I emptied my five-shot Browning, and Gayle emptied her three-shot Remington. The birds continued to struggle airborne out of the snow long enough to give me time to load two more shells and fire them. When the barrage was over, we had three roosters dead in the snow with their brilliant plumage glistening like beacons. Gayle had shot the beak away of one on a crossing shot, and I had downed two on straight-aways. Not very good percentage shooting, but what an experience!

Now whenever I approach that same corner in the draw, I stop and remember fondly that golden moment so many years ago. The wild plum trees have grown so high that you no longer can see over them, and that dear girl with the 20-gauge has been gone since 1985, claimed by an inoperable brain tumor.

However, laying all emotions aside, that experience was proof positive that pheasant hunting is also a gals' sport.

Two winners, my older son, Jay, and Jack, on a warm day in Osborne County, Kansas, when the quail proved to be more numerous than ring-necks. November 1984.

BOWEL PROBLEMS, A MAVERICK BRITTANY, AND A LIMIT OF PHEASANTS

Richard Cooper, 1990

CALL IT the back-door trots, the green-apple quick step, or any of a vast number of colorful descriptions, but when diarrhea strikes, it has the ability of getting your immediate attention and taking priority over all other activities.

For my friend, Bill Glenn, it cost him the likelihood of getting his limit of pheasants on a mild late October day in 1990 in Ringgold County, Iowa.

We were hunting on a farm which had been one of our favorite spots for several years. Bill's Brittany, Ben, was up to his usual high jinks, ranging too far out in front of us and feigning deafness when Bill tried to call him in. We knew that he was headed toward the south end of the field we were hunting, so we decided to head in that direction and possibly we could round him up.

Based on Bill's threats, Ben would have been a very bruised pooch if his owner had been able to get his hands on him. However, the irrefutable call of nature intervened on Ben's behalf, and Bill retreated to a sheltered area behind a barn to answer the urgent call. He urged Don and me to proceed south to the farm's border, possibly finding Ben along the way, and then to walk eastward along the south boundary until reaching the road which created the eastern boundary. He would drive the Suburban around to that point and serve as a blocker at the southeast corner of the property.

As Bill described it, "I hardly got done what needed to be done before I heard shooting."

More shots rang out as he waited near the Suburban. When Don and I arrived at where he was standing, no pheasants exploded from the brush, but we had experienced a most productive walk along the field's south boundary and through a large draw. Both of us had limited with three birds apiece and had also found Ben. By then, Ben had settled down and played an important role in locating some of our birds and retrieving several. We gratefully pleaded his case and saved him from a pummeling.

The next day fortunes would change, and with Bill healthy again, he would quickly bag his limit of ringnecks. Don and I had to be content with a bird apiece. Ben would stay reasonably close and was thereby spared from another round of threats to life and limb. He would also prove his mettle as a quail dog, finding a large covey and carefully hunting out the singles. While Bill was harvesting four bobs for his dinner table, Don and I were merely blowing empty holes in the Iowa sky. For many, certainly including us, it's a tough change of pace when you switch from the lumbering ringneck pheasant to the fast and explosive bobwhite quail.

Also on the second day, Ben would further ingratiate himself to his sometimes frustrated owner as we hunted a portion of one of southwest Iowa's typically rolling corn fields. Bill and I walked through a long draw in the center of the field while Don followed a brushy fence row which eventually crossed the draw at the far end. Don got a head start on his trek and would block the end of the draw as Bill and I struggled through.

We had made it only a few yards up the draw when Bill realized Ben wasn't with us. There followed more grumblings and veiled threats against the good health of his elusive Brittany. In reality, Ben decided to hook up with Don on the fence row in a display of canine fickleness, and nothing that any of us could do was going to change his decision one iota.

Don soon began to get action in the fence row. A large rooster rattled out from behind a tree startling him to the point that he couldn't punch the safety off on his Remington 11:48. As he described it a few minutes later, he finally got off a 50-yard desperation shot. The bird hit the ground but was still very much alive and hotfooted it into some of the most dense grass and brush in the fence row. The fear of a lost crippled bird loomed as Don hustled to the point where he had seen it disappear. A few feet from that location, he found Ben locked up tight with his nose no more than a foot and a half from a huge clump of dense fescue. As he approached the rigid Brittany, John Ringneck roared out of the fescue in search of a safer hideaway. With Ben in hot pursuit, the chase covered about 15 yards with Ben emerging as the winner. He brought the still struggling rooster to Don in a near perfect retrieve.

When Bill and I reached the end of the long draw, all we knew was that Don had fired a shot. Bill was livid by this time wondering where his missing dog was, not knowing of Ben's heroics in the fence row. Don apprised us of what had happened and heaped praise on Ben thereby sparing him from another threatened thrashing.

Ben continued to hunt until the age of 12 when he died of natural causes, not from any pummeling from his frustrated owner. Bill's threats of bodily harm to his maverick Brittany were always empty threats, and that was to the benefit of our many hunting trips with him. His last years afield produced many more solid points and memorable retrieves. Good though he was, all three of us would readily concede that he still ranked behind Bill's two remarkable setters, Judy and Mandy.

One thing concerning Ben that Bill rarely raised a disparaging word about was his toughness as a fighter. He hunted with other dogs very well, but if any dog approached him in a belligerent way, that dog was a whipped dog in about 15 seconds.

Art Lamm, left, and father, Don, display ringnecks taken on a late evening hunt near Adrian, Oregon, in November 1999. Mounted northern pike in background was caught by Art several years before in Minnesota.

A LONG PERILOUS TRIP HOME

Richard Cooper, 1977

THIS IS NOT the story of a fantastically successful hunt. Instead, it is the story of a 300-mile trip under the most harrowing circumstances with hunting only an incidental occurrence. The trip was across the eastern half of Kansas and the western one-third of Missouri during the Thanksgiving weekend of 1977.

We had made the traditional "off to grandma's house" trip for a family holiday weekend with my wife's parents in Bronaugh, Missouri, driving down from our home in Sedalia the night before Thanksgiving. However, my son, Jay, and I had other plans after we finished a sumptuous Thanksgiving meal prepared as only my mother-in-law could prepare it. We had arranged to meet a teaching colleague of mine, Frank Russell, and his wife at an agreed time and place in Osborne County, Kansas, for a couple of days of pheasant hunting. My wife had already been apprised of our plan several days before, so Jay and I made the trip from Sedalia to Bronaugh in my little Datsun pickup while the rest of the family came in the family sedan.

As soon as the Thanksgiving meal was finished, Jay and I loaded up and took to the highway for what was nearly a seven-hour drive from Bronaugh. Since it was Thanksgiving, virtually all eating establishments were closed, so our supper that evening consisted of doughnuts and cocoa at a Winchell's shop in Junction City, Kansas.

Frank and his wife stayed at a motel in Russell while Jay and I put up at Art Riley's Lazy L Motel in Osborne. Art was a likeable fellow who was a transplanted Missourian, coming from a community just east of Kansas City. Don and I had stayed at his place for a number of years, and a warm relationship had developed between us.

We met Frank and Delta just before sunrise the next morning at the field where we intended to begin and entered the field behind Frank's Brittany and my orange and white setter. Delta would again be the invaluable chauffeur, picking us up at the ends of long walks and transporting Jay and I back to our truck.

Jay was about a year shy of being allowed to carry a shotgun. Therefore, he walked with us and learned from our mistakes, most of which were on my part. Frank was flawless, turning in a remarkable demonstration of shooting. Through the first two fields we hunted, four roosters got up within range in front of him, and all four ended up in his game bag. All were DOA when they hit the ground, and Frank had fired just four shots. Since the Kansas daily limit is four roosters, his pheasant hunting was finished for the day. Until about mid-afternoon, Frank continued to walk with us, positioning himself so that flushing birds would be more likely to fly in front of me. Eventually, I scratched down three ringnecks, but my shooting percentage was nowhere near Frank's perfect 100 percent.

At about three o'clock, the Russells headed back for Missouri, never ones to extend the time of a hunt. Jay and I tramped until late afternoon, dressed birds and headed back to the Lazy L. Supper at an Osborne restaurant and a good night's sleep put us in shape for a half-day's hunt the following day.

The second day was a mixture of disappointment and disgust followed by near disaster. My setter decided that close-in hunting was not for him and set his sights on the horizon. He cost us innumerable shots as he repeatedly put cackling roosters into the air far out of range. Had there been a buyer available, he would have been for sale cheap that day.

A light rain began to fall around noon, and with the miserable dog performance which we were getting and only one bird, we decided to rein things in around 2:30 and head for home. We drove behind an abandoned church near the last field we hunted to change from hunting clothes to street clothes. It was a less-than-comfortable experience, considering that for a few moments we were standing in the damp air of a late November Kansas day in our underwear.

I always carry a small thermometer with me, and before the clothing change I placed it near one of the truck's front tires more out of curiosity than anything else. After the change was completed, I looked at the temperature reading and knew immediately we were in trouble. It registered 32 degrees, freezing.

Father and son started the long drive home, feeling that at any minute we would encounter ice on the highway. We didn't have long to wait. When we had gone four miles south to Luray where we turned onto K-18, we encountered the first signs of an icy surface. I slowed to about 30 miles per hour, and sometimes less, and began what would turn out to be one of the most treacherous journeys either of us would ever take. First, however, we stopped at a service station at the Luray intersection, and I called Gayle to let her know of the predicament we were in and that we would be arriving in Sedalia much later than expected. She, along with our younger son and daughter, had returned to Sedalia that morning.

It was amazing how well my little pickup performed on such a slick surface. This was long before the era of anti-lock brakes, and the little truck was genuinely primitive by today's standards. The most important factor that kept us on the highway and out of the ditch was the speed we drove, hardly ever more than 30 miles per hour.

Other drivers had poorer judgement, and the locations of their stranded vehicles were testament to that fact. Some vehicles were in the ditch, some were upside down, and some were on the field side of the ditch beyond the border fence. There was no sign of anyone inside or around any of them, so we crept on, stopping occasionally to clear the ice from our windshield and wipers.

At Junction City, we eased out onto Interstate 70 and continued the long trip eastward, noting literally dozens of stranded vehicles along the center median and in or across the ditch on the driving lane side.

By 10:30 p.m., we were approaching Topeka and listening to WIBW on the truck radio to ease the tension. WIBW is an AM station with a blowtorch signal which blankets the entire state of Kansas, day or night. In 1977, CBS Radio had revived an hour of late-night drama, the type of stimulating programming which I had listened to faithfully as a kid. WIBW carried the program, so on a veritable sheet of ice we crept through what is nearly downtown Topeka on I-70, listening intently to "Mystery Theater" and enjoying every minute of it.

The hours and miles continued to creep by. By the time we reached Kansas City, the road was somewhat better, and highway crews had made some progress in treating the icy surface. We continued our slow pace on I-70 until reaching U.S. 65 at Marshall Junction where we embarked on the last leg of the journey. Seventeen more miles, and we were home.

Gayle and the kids had long since gone to bed, trusting that the two of us would have enough good judgment and good fortune to make the trip safely. That trust proved to be accurate, but it was still a long, perilous trip home.

What was normally an eight-hour trip on dry pavement had become a harrowing experience requiring over 13. Sure, it was filled with stress, lots of it, but the combination of a father and son adventure along with "Mystery Theater" made it an experience to remember fondly for years to come.

Richard Cooper, left, and Frank Russell with Ginger, Richard's first bird dog, and a limit of Kansas bobwhites, November 15, 1969. It was so dry that the weeds would hardly grow in north-central Kansas.

THE HAT TRICK ON RINGNECKS ... IT WORKS!

Don Lamm, 1990

SOME TEN YEARS AGO, my wife, Connie, and my then 33-year-old son, Bob, decided to try our luck on a three-day pheasant hunt in Iowa, about 30 miles north of the Missouri border. I had been on one ringneck hunt with Connie a couple of years after we had gotten married in 1977, and she had demonstrated her walking staying power and her ability to shoot, and I was proud of her.

On this 1990 adventure, I had my best bird dog, Brownie, a three-year-old English setter, and Bob had Homer, a six-year-old Black Lab; Kate, a three-year-old Black Lab, and little Buster, a two-year-old hustling Springer Spaniel. Buster was a veteran in rooting out downed wounded birds in heavy switch grass, while Homer was a specialist in trailing birds for long distances, pinpointing them and finding any wounded ones which ran away when hurt but not stopped when shot. Kate was adroit in locating birds close in, and she very seldom bumped any of them prematurely, as was the case with Brownie. All of the dogs were experienced with bobwhites.

We usually road-hunted until ten in the morning, then walked the fields and draws till noon, ate lunch and again trudged them till three. We road-hunted the last hour and a half until 4:30 p.m., when we had to wrap it up. In Iowa, hunters cannot begin shooting until 8 a.m. and must quit at 4:30 p.m. and are allowed a take of three birds per day per hunter for a possession limit of nine. In Kansas, on the other hand, hunters may commence as soon as they can distinguish a rooster from a hen, which is usually about five minutes until 7 a.m., and can keep going the entire day until sundown. The daily limit per person is four and the possession limit is 16.

Iowa does allow hunters to road-hunt, whereas Kansas does not. Iowa does require the hunters to have their guns in their cases, zipped up tightly while traveling, but Kansas does not.

31

When we began road-hunting on the first day, within a half an hour, Bob spotted a rooster in some low brush which Connie and I hadn't seen. Bob executed his famous hat-tossing trick on the unsuspecting bird. Upon spotting him, he threw his orange hat out his Suburban window into the dirt road where he was and kept on driving rather than stopping the vehicle and bailing out to attempt a shot. He drove up the road a block or so and let Connie and I out. Then he turned around, drove past the pheasant, slowing down not one iota. Then he stopped 70 or 80 yards away from the bird, and he and his dogs got out. Connie and I had Brownie with us.

We began rapidly walking towards each other so as to pinch the ringneck. Upon arriving within 60 yards of each other we knew we had him within range, no matter where he went when he broke cover. Since we were quite certain he hadn't run out into the field, we knew that either Bob or Connie and I would get shots, and soon. Such was the case, and when the cackling rooster rumbled out Connie crumpled him at 25 yards with her A5 Browning 12-gauge semi-automatic, a gun with which she was adept at shooting doves. See my story "Outdone By My Wife's Gun," in this book.

Forty-five minutes later, Connie said she saw a pheasant in the bottom of a road ditch, and the process described above was repeated, only this time I downed the bird, and Brownie ran it 20 yards before she caught and held it. During the rest of the day we walked fields and road hunted later in the afternoon. We each limited out with our three birds and had excellent dog work.

On day two, we nailed a couple of more roosters by utilizing the hat trick, and Connie sighted one of them in some cedars, Bob the other. Also on the second day, at about 10:30 a.m., we were working an osage orange fence row in a field, and Buster skidded to an abrupt stop and remained as stiff as a board. Brownie and Kate pulled up behind her backing like two stationery statues. When the pheasant catapulted out, it zoomed upward rapidly and Connie and I both fired our 12s, only wounding him. Bob, being on the far side of the fence row, didn't get a chance to shoot. We observed the bird closely as he glided down and settled into the middle of the next field 225 yards away, which contained lespedesa and half knee-high weeds.

Here's where Bob's professional dog training came to be indispensable. He squared Homer up, directly in line with the bird, blew his whistle and sent him after it. The dog stopped 75 yards short, turned around, and Bob hand-waved him on. When Homer arrived in the general area of where the rooster had first landed, he stopped again when Bob blew his whistle and looked around. Then with hand signals, Bob was able to maneuver Homer closer and closer to exactly where John Ringneck had lit. Soon, the dog picked up the bird's scent and was off like a greyhound and came up with it in his mouth 50 yards from where it had gone down. An incredible retrieve followed!

The only retrieve I have ever seen superior to Homer took place a few years earlier when Buck, Bob's big Golden Retriever, dragged a large goose back to the blind which had gone down in the middle of a 120-acre cornfield across the road from Turkey Creek Farm Inc., a goose club in which I belonged. Buck's retrieve was well over 250 yards and was witnessed by several of the club members, and they talked about it for years. Buck was also hot on locating and retrieving pheasants. Once he even barreled right upon a farmer's front porch and through his yard after a bird which had been shot by Bill Glenn a hundred or so yards out in the man's field. Buck could do it all and always had himself under immaculate control. He was a master at marking birds down and won many field trial honors in his 11 years of life. When Buck did die from heart failure, it was one of the saddest days of Bob's life, as was also the case when little Buster died at age four from the same problem.

On that last day, when I had racked up two roosters and still had one to go, Bob was in the same situation. Bob pulled up to a draw in his Suburban which ran parallel to the road and which he said had yielded some John Ringnecks in the past. During this hunt, he had channeled me a time or two into predicaments where he had gotten two or three shots where I hadn't, and Connie and I began to feel perhaps we were getting "snookered."

On this particular setup, Bob told me he'd take me to the other end of the draw and I could come down through it with Brownie while he waited at the end closest to the vehicle and blocked. Then he might walk up with his dogs part of the way to meet me. Connie whispered to me, "Do the opposite of what he says." So I explained to Bob that I preferred that he go to the far end of the draw while Connie and I stayed closer to the lower end. He reluctantly agreed, and I took him there in his vehicle and returned.

Upon stepping across the road ditch and into the beginning of the draw, Brownie picked up bird smell and stiffened into a solid point in the midst of some cattails. A couple of steps launched a big rooster which rocketed out right under my feet momentarily startling me half to death. However, I recovered rapidly enough to smack him at 25 yards, and Brownie was on him like lightning.

Bob didn't get up any birds coming down the draw, and when he reached Connie and me, he remarked, "Dad, you spiked the ringneck I saw here in this spot last week. Congratulations!"

Well, we each bagged our three pheasants on the second day, and on the last, using the hat trick seven times on the trip. With the possession limit being nine birds each, we returned home with 27 ringnecks, and also we connected with 11 bobwhites which enhanced our take. Thus, we were ecstatic with a completely satisfying outing, knowing that the dogs had a great time too.

The principal lesson to be learned in this story is that when road hunting for roosters the hat pinpoints the spot where the bird is, and the pinch exerted upon the bird from hunters closing in on it from both directions is the key to success. Coming to an abrupt stop in one's vehicle when spotting a bird and then attempting to bail out right on top of him gives him too much time to run away or flush before you can get prepared to shoot.

It was a great year for pheasants in Iowa in 1982. Don Lamm bagged this limit of roosters before noon near Diagonal.

WHAT ARE FRIENDS FOR?

Richard Cooper, 1985

A TWO-DAY HUNT in southwest Iowa in early December 1985 was an example of two friends trying to help another friend in distress. I was the other friend, and I had gone through the devastating experience of losing my wife of 28 years to a brain tumor just one month before.

The two friends were Don Lamm and Bill Glenn of Sedalia who had been my regular hunting companions for the previous 22 years. Both were pallbearers at Gayle's funeral.

With my withdrawal from the regular hunting routine, they planned a pheasant hunt with one of Bob's guiding colleagues, Jim Meyer, during a time of heavy snow when the guiding business was very slack. Bob was detained elsewhere and couldn't make the trip.

Since there was limited space in Jim's Suburban which was packed with dog cages and equipment, there was only space for him and two more people. As the time of the hunt approached, they decided to try to lure me out of the house and back into the pheasant fields as an act of therapy. Bill played the role of the dropout, feigning a need to attend his daughter's birthday party.

I thought about it for a couple of days and then sought the opinion of Gayle's sister who had been of enormous help in managing all the difficult details surrounding Gayle's death. "Go for it," she said, "Life goes on, and you need to start moving with it again."

With that recommendation, I signed on for the trip, and the morning of December 7 found us trudging through six inches of snow between Lenox and Clearfield, Iowa. The wind had blown the snow into ditches and sheltered areas to depths of at least three feet so it was a hunting experience in what seemed like a different world.

I took my two setters along, and Don took one of his. However, all of them spent the first day in their cages, as the only dog we used was Jim's handsome golden retriever. We kept him busy locating and bringing back nine roosters, which is the daily limit for three hunters in Iowa. Several of them came bursting from the snow almost at the tip of our boots.

Some of the snow melted, so the second day was more suitable for pointing dogs. We allowed our frustrated setters to have free range of the snow-covered fields, and they enjoyed it to the utmost. Granted, they flushed a number of pheasants ahead of us well out of range, but there were so many birds in that part of Iowa in 1985 that we had little difficulty in filling out another day's limit.

That second day also provided Jim with the opportunity to prove beyond any doubt that he was the champion of champions in spotting roosters in the brush. He could see them in ditches and under cedars when both of us could detect nothing. In one remarkable instance, he spotted a ringneck against the background of a snow bank which must have been nearly a quarter of a mile distant, a bird which eventually ended up in one of our game bags.

It was a highly successful two-day outing, but in terms of its intended objective of pulling me out of my deep depression of the past month, it failed. I was miserable throughout and returned home with a feeling of regret that my participation in the hunt was defiling to Gayle's memory.

That feeling would change in the months ahead as I emerged back into the flow of life's activities again. Possibly the two days in the snows of Iowa provided a therapy of which I was not consciously aware.

There is one thing of which I can be unmistakably certain. Two of my closest friends tried to help me at a time when I needed help the most. For that effort, I will always be grateful.

IT AIN'T FAIR

Richard Cooper, 1996

AT TIMES there is simply no justice in the events that transpire during a pheasant hunt. Often a person finds himself in the wrong place at the wrong time when birds take to the air, but an occurrence at the end of a three-day hunt in 1996 completely eclipses that type of disappointing experience.

We parked at the last field to be hunted before heading for home. Three of us piled out, ready to make a sweep up a brushy draw which divided a 160-acre switch grass field into northwest and southeast halves. Although we had grown tired, we were still ready to give this last field a good effort, except for the fourth member of our party. Don informed us that he had flatly had it. He was going to remain in the Suburban and grade some test papers which he had brought along from one of his college classes. If any roosters were going to be bagged from this field, it would be up to us. With some quiet grumbling, the three of us set out.

Besides me there was my older son, Jay, who is built like a fullback and able to bull his way through brush and switch grass all day long. Also, there was Bob Edmondson, a retired teaching colleague of ours who now works a full schedule as a crop insurance adjuster. Bob is a classic example of the benefits to be enjoyed by following a lifelong physical fitness regimen. Now well into his seventies, he is still the freshest member of the party at the end of a day's hunt. He replaced Bill Glenn on our pheasant safaris after Bill was forced to the sidelines with an arthritic hip.

The switch grass was heavy, and by the time we got to the northeast corner of the field we were near exhaustion. So was Bob's aging Brittany, Duke. With Don back in the vehicle, we were also short one dog since we didn't want to take Zip along because she would have no master to return to. Don offered her, but we wisely declined.

I no longer had a dog to contribute to a hunt, having been without one since my last setter died of the complications of old age in the late 1980s. I thought it unwise to replace her since my hunting activities were declining, and I had no place to keep a dog at the home which my new wife and I had bought in Lamar. Renting space in a kennel seemed cost prohibitive.

As we forged our way forward about midway through the field, Bob and Jay bagged a rooster apiece. I continued to be in the wrong place each time.

On one or two occasions, we heard shots behind us, but they seemed to come from an adjoining field, and we thought nothing of it.

After completing our sweep up the brushy draw and resting for a spell, we swung to the right and walked through the southeast half of the field back to where Don was grading papers. Our decision to hunt that half was probably influenced primarily by the fact that the switch grass was slightly thinner and shorter in that part of the field.

When we were within sight of the Suburban, we could see Don was outside, and so was Zip. Upon arriving, Don told us that he had decided to take a brief walk up each side of the field for about 75 yards, carefully staying in the short grass along the edge. We had parked at the corner of the field. He had flushed and gotten not one or two roosters, but three. When put with his bird from earlier in the morning, that filled out his four-bird limit.

It ain't fair. It just ain't fair.

A FAMILY AFFAIR

Richard Cooper, 1999

I HAVE TWO SONs, Jay and Eric, and I have hunted with them countless times. However, not until mid-November of 1999, was I able to get all three of us together on the same trip. Something always seemed to interfere in past years in plans to make a trip a father and two-son event.

There are less than three years difference in the boys' ages so when they were in their early to middle teens, Boy Scout activities sometimes intervened, or in their later teen years work schedules would prevent one of them from going. When Eric went off to college at Missouri Southern State College in Joplin, such a trip seemed more remote than ever and finally was virtually put out of reach when he joined the Missouri Highway Patrol.

Nevertheless, I still harbored the idea of getting both of them on a hunt together even after Eric was assigned to the Mansfield/Mountain Grove area of south-central Missouri. Then the family responsibilities that come with a marriage and finally two children made it seem that I had only a hopeless dream. In the meantime, Jay and I, along with Don Lamm and Bob Edmondson, were experiencing great pheasant hunts in north-central Kansas. Since Jay is not married, he didn't have family responsibilities, and my wife didn't object since these were family events.

Finally in the summer of 1999, I detected a spark of interest in Eric's voice when I brought up fall hunting during a telephone conversation. I pressed forward on the matter, and he said that he would see what the vacation schedule looked like in November. In the meantime, I asked Becky, his wife, if she would strenuously object if I would take him away from the family for about three days to pursue ringnecks in Kansas. She responded that he needed to get away

The Cooper men together for the first time on a pheasant hunt in Osborne County, Kansas, on a warm November 13, 1999.

from his work schedule for a change of pace and concluded by saying, "Go for it!"

Some negotiations with his fellow troopers finally resulted in clearing enough time to make the trip.

On the Thursday evening before the season opened on Saturday, the boys drove to my home in Lamar and spent the night. The next morning, my wife served up a huge breakfast which kept our systems fueled for most of the day.

In unseasonable 70-degree warmth, we loaded into my pickup and headed out for what would be nearly a seven-hour drive to Russell, Kansas. We were joined there by Don, Bob, and Walt Diehl of Mexico, Missouri. Walt was a teaching colleague many years ago and is now retired. The weather throughout Kansas turned out to be just as warm as when we left Lamar, and it would remain so during the entire time we hunted.

The Kansas Wildlife and Parks Department had predicted that the north-central counties would be the state's pheasant hot spot in 1999, and the accuracy of their prediction was confirmed by the great number of birds we encountered.

Eric had not hunted pheasants since a trip to north Missouri with me years ago. Most of his shooting in recent years had been limited to firing range practice with his patrol issued pistol. The long layoff from shotgun use didn't seem to handicap him. By early afternoon of the first day, he had his limit of four roosters with his 12-gauge Remington 870.

Jay had his limit at about the same time using his little 20 gauge Ithaca-SKB XL900. Loaded with a 3-inch shell, the XL900 is one of the most deadly shotguns that can be used on pheasants, and Jay handles his very well.

In the meantime, the old man scratched down two roosters to barely maintain respectability.

On the second day, Jay and Eric limited again while the old man struggled in with his usual two.

The third day was devoted primarily to quail since north-central Kansas was mixed bag country in 1999. We all shared in a good harvest of bobwhites, and again Jay and Eric were top guns.

Getting one's limit is never the paramount objective of a hunt. On this trip, it was even farther down the list of objectives, even though Jay and Eric got the magic four on each of the first two days. For the Cooper clan, it was simply a great family affair.

GREAT FATHER-IN-LAW, GREAT HUNT

Richard Cooper, early 1970s

MANY PEOPLE complain about their in-laws, but that was always the least of my problems. In fact, there was no problem at all. I must have had the world's greatest mother-in-law and father-in-law, and I loved both of them deeply.

No one could dislike Mel Shearburn, as he had the kind of folksy personality that won over everyone who knew him. When we first met, I knew that ours would be a special relationship. He loved to hunt quail!

He soon became one of my absolutely favorite hunting companions, and we had many memorable quail hunts together over the years. None was quite as memorable as the late-November day in the early 1970s when we hunted in Worth County, Missouri, and inadvertently violated the state's *Wildlife Code*.

Mel had just retired, and there was finally time to take him on his first pheasant hunt. However, by then his walking stamina was greatly limited by circulatory problems, and the long treks required of pheasant hunting were simply too much for him. I hatched the idea of taking him on a quail hunt in Worth County very near the Iowa line where I had permission to hunt on two large adjoining farms. There were a few pheasants on the farms, and Mel might just be able to bag one. As it turned out, that was not to be, but we had the quail hunt of a lifetime.

It was Thanksgiving, and my family and I had driven down to my wife's parents' home in the small town of Bronaugh, Missouri, to spend the holiday. It was after a huge traditional Thanksgiving meal that I trotted out the idea of a Worth County hunt. Mel quickly latched onto the idea, and we headed out at five o'clock the next morning on what would turn out to be over a four-hour trip.

42

Although we saw very few pheasants, the two farms turned out to be a quail bonanza, and by shortly after noon we were just one bird shy of having our limits. That was in the glory days of Missouri quail hunting when the daily limit was ten.

As a light rain began to fall, Mel said nine birds were more than enough for him, so we headed for the truck which was parked inside one of the farms on an equipment road. As we began storing our shotguns, I noticed my gold and white setter settling onto point in a nearby fence row. By that time, we had birds scattered nearly everywhere. I told Mel that his tenth bird was just a few yards away and that we should go after it. Reluctantly he consented, but only on the condition that I accompany him on the opposite side of the fence row and shoot if the bird got up on my side. Obviously, he was growing tired.

Sure enough, a bird exploded from the deep brush on my side, and I dropped it at about 30 yards. I turned to my weary hunting companion and said, "Sorry, Mel, he was on my side." Looking through the dense brush, I could see Mel smile as he replied, "What bird? I dropped him out here in the field on MY side." Obviously, we had kicked out two birds from the point, shot simultaneously and got them both.

As the rain began to increase, two weary but happy hunters crowded into my little Datsun and headed for Bronaugh, and one of us had violated the Missouri *Wildlife Code*.

The next day a sumptuous quail feast was enjoyed by all, prepared as only my mother-in-law could prepare it.

MEL'S COAT

Richard Cooper, 1970s

As EACH HUNTER looks back through his mental storehouse of years of hunting experiences, strange little incidents have a way of becoming imprinted indelibly in his memory. One that I shall carry with me as long as I live is the changing color of the hunting coat of my princely father-in-law, Mel Shearburn of Bronaugh, Missouri.

Gayle and I had given it to him for his birthday in July, in plenty of time for him to use when the quail season opened in November. With each of our quail hunts that fall, the coat became a shade or two lighter, until by late season it was somewhere between gray and light tan. I finally inquired about the change of color, and Mel replied, "Oh, Lee Earl has just washed it to death." Regardless of that unusual name, she was my mother-in-law, and she had a passion for cleanliness. Mel was just too nice a guy to restrain her good intentions and tell her not to throw it in the washer after each hunting trip.

Of course, all hunters know that hunting coats should NEVER be washed. Only if absolutely necessary, a damp cloth should be used to spot clean the garment. In addition to color and water repellency, washing removes a certain familiar bond that each hunter has with his coat.

ELATION AND SADNESS FOR US ON PEARL HARBOR DAY

Don Lamm, 1941

A HUNT THAT WILL REMAIN embedded in my memory as long as I live took place on my father's and uncle's 1100-acre farm just west of Sedalia, Missouri. The farm was known by everyone as Lamm Brothers, and it was loaded with bobwhite quail. This total acreage had at least 12 to 15 coveys of birds on it and all of them were large with 18 or more bobs in each one.

In fact, for years, until it was bull-dozed out, there was a nice covey in a hedge row on the farm along the road that bordered the west side of the Missouri State Fair grounds in Sedalia, and also there was a covey in almost every other hedge row on the entire spread, and there were a good many hedge rows. My father and uncle largely respected my wish that the hunting privileges would be almost entirely restricted to the farm employees, few of whom ever hunted, and my selected friends and myself.

About eight o'clock on the morning of December 7, 1941, two 15-year-old boys, Bill Glenn and myself, and Bills's uncle Cecil Glenn, age 44, and an avid quail hunter, got out of Cecil's hunting vehicle with Cecil's five-year-old male Llewellyn English setter, Duke, and my two-year-old female Spanish pointer, Blackie. We were only a little over a mile from the Sedalia city limits, and we were poised to hunt the best part of the farm, where both Bill and I knew where there were four good-sized coveys within less than a half-mile from the car.

Cecil had taken Bill and me out bird hunting before near Beaman, Missouri, and with his model 1897 Winchester 12-gauge pump, he was a superb shot, often bagging his limit of bobs with 12 shots or less, and his dog was his equal in performance, finding, pointing and retrieving the quail perfectly in grand style.

My dog, Blackie, was quite good at pointing the birds and holding them and locating dead ones, but she wouldn't retrieve. I had gotten her free from one of my classmates in high school. In addition to her love of pointing quail, she loved to chase jackrabbits of which there were a few on the farm at that time. However, she didn't do it enough to impair the bird hunting.

Bill was shooting a double-barreled 20-gauge English Shapleigh King Nitro, and I was toting my single shot Iver Johnson 20-gauge which my father had purchased for me at Hoffman Hardware in Sedalia for seven dollars and fifty cents and had given it to me on my 12th Christmas. Also, there was very little, if any, sales tax in those days.

The hunt went well, and within ten minutes Duke came down solid on point, and Blackie, who backed well, froze, too. The birds exploded about ten yards in front of us, and both Cecil and Bill got one. I came up empty. A few minutes later we got another point, and this time I bagged one of two birds which flushed, and Cecil nailed the other, Bill being out of position to get a clear shot. Some time later, Bill and Cecil then shot a couple of more bobs out of this covey, and after that we decided to move over to another field and make contact with a new bunch of birds.

It didn't take too long to find the second covey and it, being out on relatively open ground, flushed about 50 yards away, and without any points by either dog to alert us. I cut down on them and, lo and behold, dropped one at 60 yards, a phenomenally long shot! Both Bill and Cecil were amazed and asked me what choke my gun was. I said, "Well, I don't really know, I have never checked it." Cecil then asked to see the gun, and upon looking it over carefully he exclaimed that it had a full choke, which was the wrong one for quail.

So, here I had been hunting for almost three years, an uninformed teenager, with a cheap, single-shot, full-choked gun with a hammer-haired trigger, and hadn't even realized that I needed a much better shotgun with an improved cylinder barrel and provisions for more than one shot. That single-shot gun had given me one advantage though. I had learned that every shot I took had to be taken very carefully and, as a result, I missed less often percentagewise than I would have had I had a double barrel, pump or automatic.

To make a long story short, we found two more coveys, and Bill and Cecil achieved their limits of ten birds before I did, with my having eight. We hunted another 30 or 40 minutes, and Duke locked in on point and Bill and Cecil encouraged me to shoot carefully. The bird fell between 35 and 40 yards out from the point since I had to shoot more accurately with the single shot and also, since my gun was fully choked, I had to shoot the bird farther out to keep from making mince meat out of it. The finale came just a short while later when Blackie wheeled in on a bird, steadied up like a rock, and it was added to my bag for number ten.

We started back to the car and witnessed three or four more points in which we couldn't shoot. Upon reaching the car, after loading up the dogs, we got in and commenced eating some sandwiches and drinking some soda pop. We reviewed our hunt for a little while full of enthusiasm and elation at all three of us having gotten our limit. Then Bill flipped on the car radio expecting to hear some music, but instead a news broadcaster was announcing that the Japanese had just devastated Pearl Harbor in a sneak attack by planes from aircraft carriers and had destroyed at least one-third of our Navy, plus other crucial military installations in the Pacific. We were shocked beyond belief and deeply saddened.

Less than three years later , following our graduation from high school in 1944, Bill was in the U.S. Army Air Corps in the third photo reconnaissance squadron over Japan, and I became a signalman in the U.S. Navy and served in the Panama Canal Zone. Twelve to 15 of our friends were killed in the horrible conflict, and Bill lost a close relative in the Philippines who grew up with both of us in our neighborhood.

After World War II was over, Bill and I continued to hunt both quail and pheasants together for years. Dick Cooper, a colleague of mine in the social science department at Smith-Cotton High School, Sedalia, Missouri, and co-author or this book, joined us in our frequent quail hunts in 1962 and introduced us into ringneck hunting that same year and in l963, in Kansas and Nebraska respectively.

In 1976, the three of us were out quail hunting on the same farm west of Sedalia when Bill suddenly asked me, "Don, do you remember what we were doing 35 years ago today?"

I thought and thought and finally replied, "I haven't the slightest clue." He remarked that we were doing the same damned thing we were doing right then, only it was Pearl Harbor day.

Of course, about a year after our Pearl Harbor day hunt, at age 16, I traded in my "cherished" Iver Johnson single-shot 20-gauge and bought a new Ithaca light 16-gauge pump. This gun worked fairly well, except that it occasionally threw shells on the ground instead of in the chamber when it was pumped. Just before I graduated from the University of Michigan in 1951, I got a Remington 11-48 12-gauge semi-automatic firearm which was one of the best guns I ever owned. That gun at that time only cost me $148 new.

In 1962, I purchased a Browning A5 12-gauge semi-automatic for $325 new which I still shoot today along with my Binelli twelve gauge semi automatic, which is a magnificent firearm. One of the greatest thrills a hunter can experience is the purchase of a new gun, or better yet, to receive one as a gift from his or her spouse.

In my gun collection, one of my most cherished ones is a near new model 1897 Winchester 12-gauge pump which I bought in honor of Cecil Glenn, who took such a keen interest in us teenagers. As the truant officer for the Sedalia school system for 40 years, he helped many a boy and girl achieve success, whereas without his competent and caring guidance they may have gone astray.

Also, a year after I purchased my A5 Browning 12-gauge semi automatic, Bill bought himself one, and it had a particularly beautiful walnut stock of which he was very proud and which was the envy of those who saw it just after he purchased it. On his first hunt with the gun, while with Dick Cooper and me east of Sedalia, within five minutes after he had gotten out of the car, Bill stumbled over a hidden log hidden in the grass while chasing his dog. Both he and the gun hit the ground with a hard thump.

Upon getting up somewhat bruised, he looked at his gun, and the expression on his face looked as though the world had come to an end for there was a deep three-inch long gouge in the stock, and it is still there today as a reminder of what one goes through sometimes to bag those cotton pick'n birds!

A HIT HIS FIRST TIME AT BAT

Richard Cooper, 1981

EVERY MINOR LEAGUER who is brought up to the majors dreams the same dream before he plays in his first game — a hit his first time at bat — provided, of course, that he isn't a pitcher.

My son, Eric, accomplished the equivalent when he went on his first quail hunt with me — a downed and retrieved bird on his very first shot.

It was a Sunday afternoon in mid-November 1981, and Eric had turned 12 just a few weeks before. My wife and I hadn't purchased a shotgun for him as yet, so I let him use my Franchi 20-gauge semi-automatic, a good gun for a kid his size. In fact, it's a fine gun for anyone to use on quail or pheasants because of its light weight (5-1/2 pounds) and easy handling, even after a long day in the field. There is no doubt, it's my all-time favorite for ringnecks.

It was a fine day for bird hunting, cloudy with the temperature climbing into the lower 50s by early afternoon and hardly any wind at all.

Eric was enthusiastic about his first "real" hunt as we loaded my two setters, Pride and Troop, into the back of my truck. He had gone along on a number of trips before, but this would be his first time as an active participant.

We headed out northwest of Sedalia to one of our favorite places, a farm a few miles north of the small community of Dresden. It usually had several coveys on it, and we had heard that another well-known quail hunter in Sedalia had located five coveys just on the west side about a week before.

One good thing about the owner, he granted hunting privileges to most anyone who would observe his rules. Basically, they were staying out of the field where he had cattle, closing all gates when going through them and taking quail in moderation. Any sensible

The day Eric (12) scored on his very first shot at a quail. Near La Monte, Missouri, November 15, 1981.

hunter should have no trouble complying with such reasonable regulations.

Basically, there were two parts of the farm where quail could be found, to the west of the farm house and to the southeast of the house.

We decided to try the area where the aforementioned hunter had not been the week before. We parked along the one-eighth mile road leading into the house and let the dogs out of their cage to work out the kinks, along with other substances with which they desired to part.

With all in readiness, we plunged into the brush behind the dogs, hoping for a quick covey find. Eric brimmed with enthusiasm as he hoped to fire at a live quail for the first time. I had prepared him for this moment by having him shoot some hand trap on a number of occasions. Now, it was the big leagues.

We didn't have long to wait. My veteran setter, Pride, soon gave signs that she was near some birds, and after trailing them for a minute or so settled down on a solid point along the brushy edge of a creek. This was Eric's big moment. I told him to be ready and to walk slowly forward behind the rigid dog. I would sit this covey rise out unless a bird should fly out behind us. When he got about to the dog's shoulder, a covey of about 10 birds exploded from the brush and headed out in the direction of a pond to our left. As far as I could tell, Eric followed his earlier instructions to the letter, swinging the little Franchi onto the escaping birds and singling out just one of them. The 20-gauge spoke with a surprisingly loud roar, and a bird dropped out in the middle of the field. Pride bounded out to pick it up and bring it back to a beaming 12-year-old. A base hit the first time at bat.

That would be the first bird of a remarkably successful afternoon's hunt. Pride and Troop would find four more coveys, one with about 20 birds in it. Eric got only one more bird, as he found that missing bobwhites became quite easy. It would require more time and a lot of self-discipline before he could consistently repeat that first memorable shot. Over the years that would come, and many enjoyable quail hunts were the result.

However, that first shot over Pride's point would remain permanently etched in our memories. One for one in the big leagues.

EVERY HUNTER DESERVES A GREAT DOG

Richard Cooper, 1975

I HAVE OFTEN HEARD it said that every dedicated quail hunter deserves at least one great dog during his lifetime. I couldn't agree more. Two of my three closest hunting companions had such good fortune, and so did I. The third companion was my father-in-law, Mel Shearburn, and he probably came close. He acquired a Brittany with tremendous promise, but it was so late in Mel's hunting career that the dog didn't have an opportunity to develop as he should. The dog was loaned out to other hunters and was allowed to develop bad habits which blunted his chances of developing to his full potential.

My great English setter, Jack, brings home the bacon during a late season quail hunt near Hughesville, Missouri, January 5, 1975.

My friend, Bill Glenn of Sedalia, was blessed with two outstanding dogs during his years of hunting. One was a rangy female setter which possessed a nasty disposition toward other dogs, but when involved in the business of hunting possessed a sharp nose, steadiness of point and a determination to retrieve every bird which was downed no matter where it fell, in the middle of a creek or in a brush pile. There wasn't a retrieving obstacle which Judy couldn't overcome. He acquired her from a kennel in a small eastern Kansas town just outside of Kansas City after answering a classified ad for registered setter puppies in the *Kansas City Star*. Tragically, Judy was run over by a school bus when she was only five years old, so no one knows how great a dog she may have become.

Bill's second great dog was also a female setter, but any similarity to Judy ends at that point. Mandy was a small, even-dispositioned dog who could cover ground like a pointer when she was of a mind to. She had an outstanding nose and would hold a point as long as the bird she had found stayed put. Her retrieves were nearly flawless. She continued to hunt with boundless endurance through her 12th year, but the next season saw her slowing considerably. That turned out to be her last season, and she went into a well-earned retirement.

Mandy was not a registered dog. Bill got her for free from a local Sedalia family which had her as a pet and felt that a small baby and a four-month-old puppy might not go well together. A newspaper ad saying "free to a good home" led to over 12 years of memorable quail hunting.

If you're a field trialer or a breeder of dogs, registration papers may be important, but for the average bird hunter, papers mean very little. What is important is a good nose, staunchness of point, honoring other dogs on point and a willingness to search for downed birds and to retrieve them. These are what is generally referred to as "meat" dogs.

Don Lamm's great dog was out of one of the litters of English Setters from my backyard kennel. He named her Dana, and it wasn't until she was two years old that she began to show signs of being an outstanding bird finder. Hers was not a classic point, but when it assumed a certain sort of crouch, you knew she had a bird or covey almost within arm's reach. Don's son, Bob, called it her "grizzly bear" point. She was so steady that birds usually stayed put until we caught up with her. She was a very even-tempered dog until time to remove burrs at the end of a day afield. That procedure always required two people, one whose responsibility it was to hang onto her head and jaw.

My great dog was a littermate to Dana, and he was a large and rangy orange and white male. I named him Jack, copied after the name of my dad's pet pit bull which he had as a child. His point was not stylish, but it always signified that a bird or birds were close at hand, and you'd better be ready for an explosion of feathers. If you consider his entire hunting career, he wouldn't be classified as great, but he had two periods in his life when he was absolutely remarkable. The first was when he was quite young, only two or three years old, and the second was in his later years when he was eight or nine. During those years, he was a virtual hunting machine, ranging out at just the right distance, solid productive points, and soft-mouthed retrieves that left nothing to be desired. I retired him during his 11th year.

One hunt with Jack during his middle years turned out to be a near disaster. We were hunting east of Sedalia near what is known locally as Muddy Creek; it's actually a branch of the Lamine River. The weather had just turned bitterly cold, and a layer of ice had formed on the creek's surface. Jack decided to hunt the other side and started across on the ice. Fearing that it was too thin to hold him, I called him back. He had taken only a couple of return steps when my worst fears came to pass, and through the ice he went. He struggled to get back onto the ice several times, but it continued to give way under his weight. By the time he was 10 to 15 feet from shore, he was nearly exhausted from his struggles. Not knowing how deep the water was, my only recourse was to go in after him. With Bill and Don standing by to help if needed, I strode into the frozen creek, grasped Jack by his collar and headed back toward the shore. Fortunately, the water was only a little over knee deep. While they pulled me ashore with one arm, the other was firmly attached to my bedraggled setter. With a final tug, a wet hunter and dog were returned to reasonably dry land. Needless to say, the hunt was over for the day, but I had avoided losing my best dog.

While on the topic of dogs, I can't resist telling about an absurd event that occurred at the end of an extremely cold day's quail hunt in early January of 1975. We had our great triumvirate of dogs with us, Bill's Mandy, Don's Dana and my Jack. We had started the hunt on the west side of Bill's farm and concluded at a barn located below

A field of milo stubble and the rolling countryside of north-central Kansas make a perfect backdrop for displaying five ringnecks bagged by Bob Edmondson, left, and Richard Cooper in November 1998. Three of the five were taken over solid points.

his home. My truck which had a bed cover with cage inside was located far back where we had started. Since it was nearly sundown, a quick return to my truck was necessary. Bill offered the services of his old pickup which was parked near his barn, but since it had an open bed with no place to tie a dog, all of us piled into the cab for the return trip. If you haven't experienced a two-mile ride inside the cab of a pickup truck with two other people and three slightly wet dogs, you've really missed something. Also, it was proven to us beyond all doubt that dogs have no qualms about passing gas profusely. By the time we got back to my truck, both windows were open, and we were more than ready to bail out.

BIRD DOGS I'VE HAD
OVER THE PAST 60 YEARS

Don Lamm, 1940 to the present

As ANY BIRD HUNTER who has tromped the fields and woods over a long period of time knows, it is the dog work which makes the hunt. Without a dog, hunters may stumble into and bag a few birds on a long day of walking, but they miss out on the true thrill of the hunt, that is, watching the dogs point, finding the bird when it goes down and the retrieving of it as they bring the game back to their masters.

Every bird hunter can look back and vividly remember every single dog he or she has owned and can plug in either good memories or bad, depending on the nature of the dog. With this in mind, I want to tell you about the dogs I have had over 60 years of upland bird hunting.

My first bird dog was given to me when I was just turning 14 and was a freshman in high school. A close friend of mine, Charles Johnson, with whom I frequently swam in the Liberty Park swimming pool in Sedalia, Missouri, brought this solid black dog, except for a streak of white down its throat and breastbone to its forelegs, over to my parents'

Don Lamm's first bird dog, Blackie, a female Spanish pointer acquired in 1940. Blackie was a faithful and productive finder of bobwhites for ten years.

house, and I immediately fell in love with it. My parents, who always took a great interest in my activities, gave me the green light to become the owner and, of course, I named it Blackie.

Charles had given her to me free, and as she matured, Bill Glenn, another close friend of mine, and I had many a quail hunt with her on my father and uncle's 1100-acre farm just west of Sedalia. While Blackie, a Spanish Pointer, would chase jackrabbits and give them a great run for their money, she always settled down to business when it came to bobwhites, and her points were solid as a rock. Whenever she did freeze on birds, they were always there! Much more about Blackie appears in the story in this book entitled, "Elation and Sadness For Us on Pearl Harbor Day."

During her long life, Blackie got run over twice by cars and was accidentally shot once. She died in 1950 when I was a junior at the University of Michigan while I was working on my bachelor's degree in economics. She lived to be 10 years of age. During World War II, while on leave for two weeks after finishing boot camp training at Great Lakes Naval Station, I had several good hunts with her and also after the war when I came home during college semester breaks and on major holidays. Her death caused sadness for everyone in the family, for she was a house pet as well as a hunting dog, and she was almost human.

The next dog I owned was Jaynee, which I purchased in the 1960s from a well-known dog trainer in Sedalia, Mr. Griffith. She was two years old at the time, and he guaranteed me that Jaynee would perform well and never break point. He also said that she would find as many or more birds as any dog on the hunt, and he proved to be absolutely correct. A story about her entitled, "The Invisible Quail Or Was It?" is included in this book.

Jaynee was a very small setter. She had been the runt of the litter, Griffith had pointed out, but she was also very strong and solidly built. In addition, she was very tender-mouthed with birds and was a completely lovable creature who loved to hunt and could do so all day long. One fall day when she was nine years old, I took her up on the Blackwater River just north of Marshall Junction, Missouri. Accompanying me were my two sons, Art and Bob, and Bill Rose, a close friend who often hunted with us.

For years Bill was a counselor both in Sedalia's senior high and middle schools, and he always had either a good pointer or two or good Brittanies. He and I had friendly competitive contests for years on who could bring home the most doves and quail during those hunting seasons. He died in his early 60s from heart trouble, and many hunters and fishermen attended his wake and were deeply saddened at the loss.

Well, we had gotten into three coveys in the river bottom that day, and about 4:15 in the afternoon we decided to traverse some acreage on higher ground where a lot of lespedeza, which is excellent feed and cover for bobwhites, was in evidence. Bill's big liver and white pointer came down on point, and Jaynee moved up and backed. We got three birds on the covey rise and then spread out to hunt down a few of the singles. Ten minutes went by and we lost track of Jaynee, and then a half hour transpired and she still hadn't shown up and it was now dark. We called and whistled but still no Jaynee, and she wasn't back at the vehicles when we got ready to go home.

So we went back to Sedalia without Jaynee and, of course, I was very upset. Because of her small size, I envisioned her being attacked and devoured by coyotes. The next morning, Art and Bob went back to the field where she had disappeared, and they looked, called and whistled for well over an hour, but no luck. Finally, the next day, which was going on the third day she had been lost, I went by myself to the area where we had last hunted with her, and called and whistled loudly for about ten minutes.

All of a sudden, here she came running up to me, and we had a most happy reunion. Who knows, she might have been locked in on point a good part of those two days she had disappeared! She was that kind of a dog, similar to Ginger, one of Dick's first setters who would sometimes disappear on a hunt and sometime later when we caught up with her, she was staunch on point. In her prime, Ginger was one of the finest dogs I ever hunted over.

After that incident, I took Jaynee hunting a time or two more, but it was evident that she had "lost it." On one of the hunts she got out on the road and was almost run over twice. On the next hunt, she disappeared again for several hours before we found her, and this had not been her normal temperament at all prior to the Blackwater hunt. She lived out her last four years as a house pet, and her hunting days were over.

The next dog I acquired free was Dana, a black and white Llewellyn English setter. She was a large female, and during her first two years she loved to hunt, but she was exceedingly nervous and excitable. She ran through covey after covey of quail, flushing them to kingdom come, exasperating me to no end, and I told my hunting buddies, Bill Glenn and Dick Cooper, that I'd probably get rid of her. Upon hearing that, Bill said, "Give her to me; I think she has a lot of potential and she will make a fine dog." That alerted me, because I knew that Bill had trained two fine dogs which I had hunted with many times, and he had a special sixth sense about sizing up bird dogs. I told him, "I think I'll give her two or three more chances, and if she doesn't work out then I'll be happy to let you have her."

A week or so later found Bill, Dick and I hunting on Bill's 300-acre place out northeast of Beaman, Missouri, a mile or two. Bill had several nice coveys of bobwhites, and as we moved through some cover next to a group of trees along a small creek, Dana became very birdy. This time she didn't rush in like a mad man, but she didn't freeze up on point either. Dick and Bill's dogs were in back of Dana and hadn't approached closely enough to get a good whiff of the quail.

The birds got up about 15 yards from us without any of the three dogs spooking or pointing them, and when I shot twice with my A5 Browning 12-gauge semi-automatic, I got one bird for each shot, and Bill and Dick each got one. Thus, four birds bit the dust, and when Dana saw all of this happen at close range, she ran and picked up one of the birds and brought it to me. We showed her the other three birds, and one could see that she had finally gotten the connection concerning how dog and hunter needed to work together for success!

After that day, Dana seldom, if ever, broke coveys, and she became a calm, superb dog on doves, quail and pheasants. She became one of the "Big Three" dogs in the life of Bill, Dick and me. For a good ten years it was Jack, Mandy and Dana, three of the finest trio of dogs that ever set foot after upland game birds. Jack, Dick's dog, and Mandy, Bill's dog, were better than Dana all around, because they retrieved much better, but when it came to finding coveys, pointing them, and locating dead birds, Dana could well hold her own with them. She lived to be 13, and died from what I suspect to be heartworm, a horrible disease dogs get from carrier mosquitos.

This may be a terrible thing to say, but I cannot for the life of me understand why God ever put mosquitos here on earth, because they seemingly do absolutely no good whatsoever and are the carriers and causes of numerous life killing diseases in both man and animal. At least flies have some value in that they rid us of dead carrion. By the way, what applies to mosquitos also applies to ticks. In some respects they are worse than mosquitos, because they are the carriers of the virus which causes both lymes disease and rocky mountain spotted fever.

At the same time I had Dana, for a year or two I also had Tommy, a fast-moving pointer which I purchased for $300 from state senator John Ryan of Sedalia, Missouri, a close friend of our family. My idea here was to be the proud owner of both a pointer and a setter, which many hunters take great pleasure in. Tommy was good at locating birds; he did range out farther than I liked as many pointers do. He also flushed some birds before one of us could get up on him, but when he did hold a point it was one of the most stylish ones imaginable.

One day John approached me and asked me if I would sell Tommy back to him for the same amount I had given him for it a year or so earlier. I asked him why he wanted to buy the dog back, and he said that his dear friend and hunting buddy, Frank Wagner, a prominent Sedalia accountant, really liked the dog and was very unhappy when John had sold Tommy to me, and he had pleaded with him to buy him back. Since Frank and his wife were also very close friends with my parents and with me as well, I was most happy to oblige. Besides, at that time I needed some extra money as I wanted to purchase an additional gun.

Following that, I had a chance to purchase a pointer pup for $50, and I named it Copper-Promise and called it Copper for short. However, I never got to hunt this dog because its leg mysteriously got broken at the kennel where I was boarding it at the time. The leg became badly infected and got progressively worse, necessitating her having to be put away. Needless to say, I never kept another dog at that kennel again, and I immediately built two dog pens at the house where I was living that year.

In 1981, a year or so after Dana died, my son Bob gave me a one-year-old stylish brown and white female English setter which I called Flair. After I hunted her a year or two on doves, four or five times a week, she became exceptionally good at it. When she first began hunting them, she would get too far out and flush bunches all over the field and chase them. But after I became firm with her and reined her in and got her under control, she would slow down to a walk when she scented doves, and on many occasions would point them as well. She found many a wounded and dead bird in cornfields and grass that I otherwise would never have been able to put in my game bag.

During all of the 1980s and early 1990s I shot between 200 and 300 doves a season, largely with Flair's great help. She also turned out to be very steady on single quail. I never saw her make a false point on a single quail, and when it was knocked down seldom was it that she failed to find it whether dead or just wounded. However, she did flush coveys far too often and on pheasants she was fair, but not really good. Her outstanding work with doves certainly warranted her well worth keeping, and I also took her on a number of sensational pigeon shoots which she always enjoyed as much or more than I did.

When I would kill four or five pigeons, I would lay them out in a cornfield about 35 yards from some cover at the field's edge, and they served as decoys and the birds would come into them like ducks, which served to sharpen up my duck shooting in late fall when I went up to Turkey Creek Farm, Inc. The most pigeons I ever shot on any one hunt was 20. After skinning them out in the field before going home, I would later boil them and feed them to Flair and any other dog I had at that time.

At the time I had Flair, I also acquired from my life-long friend and hunting companion, Bill Glenn, who is mentioned numerous times in this book, a large male brown and white English setter which was dubbed the name of "Jumper." Bill abhorred my labeling the dog that, but the name was appropriate because when it came time to feed it each day, he would always jump way up in the air numerous times and also run and jump all over the pen.

One summer I sent both Flair and Jumper to Saskatchewan, Canada, for three months of additional training, and for a year after they got back they did a great job. The man who took them up there was Quentin Bybee of Cross Timbers, Missouri, for years and years a well known and renowned dog handler. The cost to send the two dogs for that three months of special training came to $900. Eventually, both Flair and Jumper came down with heartworm and underwent treatment. Flair recovered, but Jumper didn't make it.

Another setter which ended up in one of my two pens while I

had Flair was Donna. Bob, my son, gave her to me free gratis, and she turned out to be quite a competent bird finder and would hold them for a long time on point. However, she was one of those dogs that liked to hunt strictly on her own, and one would have to spend too much time looking for her. One day we took her out hunting south of Florence, Missouri, and my older son, Art, and one of his close friends and I shot several birds over her points, but at eleven o'clock she completely disappeared, and no amount of searching, calling or whistling brought her in.

We had to abandon the effort to find her that day, and Art's friend inquired around the area for a week or so without results. Some weeks later, a farmer called and said he had the dog at his house, having found her in his hay barn, thin and emaciated. Over a period of time she was revived, and her weight came back up to normal. She was then given to a close friend of my younger son, Bob. He said his buddy, who is a fireman in Kansas City and gets large blocks of time off because of the nature of the job, had some good hunts with her for several years before she died.

About four years before Flair died at the age of 15 in 1995, my son, Art, donated to me a brown and white female setter pup which came to be known as "Brownie." This was beyond all doubt the best bird dog I ever had. She was a "natural," minded well, worked in close which nearly every hunter appreciates a lot from a dog, found lots of birds and was superb with doves, quail and pheasants. She also held a point forever until her master was ready to flush the birds, and found wounded or dead birds like almost nothing I had ever seen before, especially for a dog so young in age.

One spring day when she was four years old, I let her out of her pen, as I usually did every day or so, in order that she could run around and get some needed exercise on my seven-acre place. She scampered around as usual, and I kept track of her for an hour or so and then became involved in some other activity. All of a sudden, I became aware that I had not seen nor heard Brownie for about an hour, and I started looking and calling for her. No results. Then I contacted all of the neighbors and ran all of the roads in the area in my car. Still no beloved dog. The next morning she wasn't in or around the pen.

I then ran ads in the local newspapers and on the radio offering a reward to anyone who found her, and for two weeks there was no response. Eventually, after another three or four days went by, a lady called me and said she thought she had my dog.

Of course, I immediately went to her house in Sedalia, full of anticipation, but instead of Brownie, she had a black and white female setter pup which she said had been at her house for five days and that she was going to take it to the humane society animal shelter the next day. Realizing by this time that I had lost Brownie for good, probably to some cloddish hunter or hunters who had stolen her or to the evil persons who steal dogs and sell them to medical research laboratories, I told the woman, "If you're going to take it to the animal shelter, give her to me and I'll give her a good home."

This she did, and I took the pup home with me. From the beginning, she was an alert, inquisitive dog with a superb nose and fast on her feet. She grew rapidly and I worked with her in the yard frequently. She was so full of energy and dash, it occurred to me, and concurred in by Dick Cooper, that Zipper would be the ideal name for her, and that is what she goes by today, except that the shortened version of "Zip" is more often used.

Zipper is now six or seven years old, and her main forte is pheasants, although she is also sharp on quail. She can cover more ground faster than any dog I've ever seen. Even in heavy switch grass, she can be a quarter of a mile away, and the next minute she will be right at one's feet! Of course, the closer she is to me, the better she points and holds; the farther out she is the more birds she bumps. The disadvantage of her being really far out in heavy cover is that she cannot be seen, and if she can be seen and she points, she will often break the bird before I can get to her.

Since I am now 73 years of age I can't move very fast due to both of my knees having been injured, causing them to be weaker than those of a normal person. One of them was severely strained as a result of my trying to jump across a ditch at age 45 while quail hunting with Dick and Bill north of Sedalia. They had to go get a pickup truck to haul me out of the woods and take me to the hospital, and I ended up being on crutches for a month and wore a brace for a year, but I was able to hunt with the brace strapped on.

When a bird is knocked down and Zip is anywhere near, she's on it at once, and I have watched her trail wounded running ringnecks a quarter of a mile and find them. When she does follow a wounded bird, I have to do my best to keep up with her because when she finds it she just stands over it and won't retrieve. Of course, once she does catch up with it and it tries to get away, she will grab it and hold on until I go to her and take it out of her mouth. Zip is also superb at trailing live pheasants, and by keeping a close eye on her and staying with her as best as I can I have made many a kill over her points.

The hunter should always watch his or her dog carefully, and many times follow it to where it wants to go rather than constantly calling it in and forcing it to always hunt closely back and forth immediately in front of him or her. After all, a good bird dog is blessed with a nose far superior to that of a human being and it, through its proboscis, can pick up bird scent much farther away than any person, if the person is able to even smell any birds at all!

The next story in this book entitled, "A Sensational Bobwhite and Ringneck Hunt In Central Kansas," illustates many of the positive characteristics and what a fantastic setter Zipper has turned out to be.

A late season bonanza in Osborne County, Kansas. Bob Lamm, Don Lamm and Jan Nielson, left to right, with part of a day's bag during a four-day hunt. Co-author Dick Cooper took this photo on December 28, 1993.

A SENSATIONAL BOBWHITE AND RING-NECK HUNT IN CENTRAL KANSAS

Don Lamm, circa 1993 or 1994

WHEN ZIP was about 14 months old, I took her on a hunt for pheasants and quail out into central Kansas. Four of us hunted for four days since the limit on pheasants was four per day per man and the possession limit was 16 per hunter. Dick Cooper and I hunted mostly for pheasants and Bob, my younger son, and his close friend, Jan Nielsen, senior carpenter at Southern Illinois University at Carbondale, concentrated principally on quail.

Since Bob guides pheasant hunters during the Iowa ringneck season for over two months almost every day, he gets tired of hunting them, and a good quail hunt is like a vacation and breath of fresh air to him. Jan is also glued to bobwhites. However, both Bob and Jan would shoot at a rooster if it got up in front of them, but they didn't actively seek them out as Dick and I did.

We had a total of eight dogs. I had Zip, and Dick and I hunted primarily with her, except when Bob and Jan joined up with us to help us drive pheasants in switch grass or attempt to corner them in some other way. Occasionally we would also join them and shoot at a few quail if they flushed in cover that looked good for roosters. Bob's four dogs included Brie, a lemon and white female six-year-old pointer; Hazel, a liver and white female five-year-old pointer; Homer, an eight-year-old male Black Lab; and Tess, a two-year-old female Black Lab.

Jan's three dogs encompassed Dolly, a nine-year-old female pointer; Spike, a nine-year-old male pointer, and Ginger, a five-year-old black and white Llewellyn English setter. Both Bob and Jan's dogs had undergone extensive training, extensive hunting constantly, and each was equipped with both beeper and electric collars. My dog, Zip, had neither.

Bob and Jan would hunt two of their dogs for a half-day, and then Bob would hunt his other two dogs the other half-day while Jan hunted his one. Both Bob and Jan had fancy dog trailers which would hold up to six dogs, and Jan fed his dogs large quantities of horse meat.

At the beginning of the hunt, Bob and Jan parked their hunting vehicles with their dog trailers on a dirt road adjacent to the acreage we intended to run the dogs over and where Dick and I knew there were at least two coveys of birds close and the possibility of a pheasant or two. Before Bob and Jan could get their hunting gear out and fasten the beeper and electric collars on their dogs, Zip had already run a hundred yards into the cornfield and came down solid on a point in a grassy area. Dick and I hustled up to cover the point and called to Bob and Jan to come over. For some reason, they dillied and dallied, and Dick and I shouted to them again.

Still they hadn't started over to us, either because they weren't entirely ready or they thought Zip, being just a little over a year old was inexperienced and was on a false point. However, Zip still held the point, and finally after five minutes Bob and Jan came up with their four dogs, and being exceptionally well trained, they froze and backed Zip's still staunch point in one of the most beautiful sights Dick and I had witnessed in our well over 50 years of bird hunting.

Upon flushing the 22-bird covey, all four of us got shots off, with Jan dropping two, and Bob, Dick and I crumpled one each. Needless to say, I was immensely proud of Zip for holding that point for a full ten minutes, giving Bob and Jan time to be on the scene for the flush.

After getting points on three more bobwhites and killing two of them, we felt that we needed to move off to another farm of 640 acres a mile or so away and locate another covey or coveys and some pheasants. We started through a mile-long draw which twisted like an anaconda snake through the middle of the property. Dick and I had hunted it many times since 1962 and knew that it contained both ringnecks and at least four large coveys of bobwhites.

About halfway through the draw, in a rocky, grassy place along a little creek bank where we had nearly always gotten up ringnecks before, all of a sudden six cacklers thundered out about 30 yards ahead of us before the Zip had gotten up to them. The birds flushed on Dick's and my side of the draw, so he and I were the ones who got the shots. My A5 12-gauge Browning semi-automatic, with its poly choke set on an improved modified pattern, barked twice on a straightaway presentation, and two roosters tumbled into the weeds within ten yards of each other at about 40 yards. Dick took a bird at about 35 yards on his right and creamed it with his SKB Ithaca three-inch chambered 20-gauge, model 900.

Dick walked over and picked up his bird, and I saw Zipper run up and stand over one of my birds, mouthing it gently to make certain that it did not get away. Since she didn't retrieve, I went up and put it my hunting coat and then began looking for the other bird which I thought would be a cinch to find since the two pheasants had fallen so close to each other.

However, an easy find was not in the cards, and an intense search was begun with Zip working back and forth in the weeds and the grass. Finally, after ten or 12 minutes, she stiffened up on a rock solid point 35 yards from where the rooster originally fell. It was buried deep in some switch grass near the edge of the cornfield which bordered the draw. I cautiously peered into the place where Zip's nose was centered, saw the bird, made certain that my gun was ready in case the bird flushed or ran, and then plunged my right hand underneath the dog's stance and grabbed the ringneck firmly. After making sure that the bird was dead, I deposited it in my gamebag and gave Zip a lot of verbal praise and scratched underneath her front legs, a mark of affection every dog loves.

Within ten minutes, on their side of the draw which had become considerably wider by now, Bob and Jan's dogs came down on point, and when the quail burst out at their feet each man got one. They proceeded to pursue them on up the draw for singles, while Dick and I took Zip and branched off into a long line of trees bordered by a lot of grass and a cornfield on the east side, ideal cover for ringnecks as past years had shown.

In 15 minutes, Zip froze solid in front of Dick, and I moved forward to back him up in case he missed. However, such was not the case, and Dick pummeled the rooster at 25 yards, which illustrates how rapidly he was able to get his light 20-gauge up and into action. In fact, on our hunts together throughout the years, he has nearly always shot 20-gauge guns and I have almost always shot 12-gauge ones. The other 20-gauge which Dick often carries with him in the field is a featherweight Franchi that chambers two and three-quarter-inch shells.

Dick's theory is that a very light gun does not wear a hunter down on a long walk nearly as much as does a heavier one; it comes up much faster, swings and handles much more smoothly, and if a bird is 35 yards or less away when it gets up, the 20-gauge's killing power is just as potent as that of a 12-gauge.

My theory is that while a 12-gauge is heavier, its shells have more pellets in each respective length of shell and a bigger pattern. Also, its killing range reaches out at least ten yards farther than a 20. Suffice it to say, when Dick and I are preparing to shoot at a bird, if it flushes up close, he nearly always creams it before I can even get my gun up halfway to my shoulder, but if it gets up farther out, I usually end up bagging it. When we finished hunting that section of land, Bob and Jan had two pheasants each and five bobwhites apiece, and Dick had three ringnecks to my two, and we each had two quail.

After eating lunch, we decided to go several miles to another big farm which Bob and Jan had hunted in years past. When we stopped to park and let the dogs out, Zip's trailer pen door was wide open and there was no dog. I was petrified, realizing that she had either jumped out or had fallen out due to the fact that the door latch had not been sufficiently secured.

Since we had traveled several miles, part of them being down a busy highway, I had visions of her lying in the middle of it run over. I told Bob and Jan to immediately take one of the vehicles and help me find her. Just as we were all ready to start back to retrace our journey, we looked up, and right in the middle of the dirt road where we had stopped to hunt, a quarter of a mile away, we saw Zip coming toward us. I blew my whistle and called loudly to her, and she came running up to me full speed. With a sigh of relief and joy I embraced her, so happy that she was still alive and well.

Next, an incident occurred which both Dick and I will never forget and which we have talked about over the years on a good number of occasions. When we started hunting, we soon encountered a curvy ditch with good weedy cover which ran through a portion of a cornfield. Jan and Bob's dogs started creeping slowly, slowly up to it, which signaled to us that birds were up ahead, probably rather close. Bob's two pointers and Jan's pointer and setter then made several false points as they crept up the ditch. While this was going on, Zip went on up ahead of them. Jan remarked that she was moving too fast and had overrun the covey and that his two dogs and Bob's would have them definitely pinpointed in less than a minute.

Dick and I had been watching Zip closely as well as Jan and Bob's dogs, and we disagreed with Jan. We said that we believed the birds were up ahead of Zip and not behind her. Just then, both Jan and Bob's dogs locked up on a solid point, but no bobwhites or ringnecks flushed. Dick and I then looked up ahead 15 yards, and there Zipper, who had made no false points or creeps, was on point, moving not a single inch, her nose riveted upon a patch of weeds seven yards directly in front of her. Jan and Bob's dogs were still farther back, but when the two men moved up to Dick and me, their dogs came up also and backed Zip's point.

Four steps forward caused the bobs to explode, and Jan and Bob each dropped one, while Dick and I drew blanks. Nevertheless, I was very proud of Zip outmaneuvering Jan and Bob's veteran canines and proving them wrong. However, both Dick and I agreed that watching those three pointers work those birds up that ditch, even though they were upended by Zip, was one of the most thrilling experiences each of us had ever beheld. Indeed, there is nothing more beautiful than watching a truly superb pointer work birds! Anyway, I wouldn't have taken five thousand dollars for Zip at that moment, even if Jan or Bob had offered it to me, which they didn't.

We then split up, with Jan and Bob going on up that ditch for more quail, while Dick and I took Zip and headed for a switch grass patch a hundred and 50 yards from them. Shortly after we got into the grass, Zip suddenly stopped dead in her tracks and froze. When the rooster whirled out of its resting place, it went out on my side, and I knocked it down at 40 yards, and Zip was on it in a flash.

This left Dick and me tied at three and three on ringnecks with a few quail for each of us as a bonus. Since the daily limit for pheasants in Kansas is four per hunter per day, we each had one more to go. We worked the switch grass some more and then headed down a swale toward another three acres of weedy cover. Bob and Jan had moved into a draw within a hundred and 20 yards from us. All of a sudden, Dick and I heard two shots over their way and then they yelled, "Get him, get him, he's headed your way!" Sure enough, the big rooster was barreling right toward us.

We ducked down so he would be less likely to see us and thus not flair off, and as a result, the bird approached within 35 yards of Dick. As Dick raised up to shoot, it began to veer off, but it was too late. Dick's SKB 20-gauge did its potent work; the pheasant folded and bounced on the ground, hard. Zip observed all of this and bounded out and stood over the bird, preventing it from getting away. Since Zip wouldn't retrieve, Dick walked over and admired the beautiful trophy, shortly thereafter tucking it into his game bag. He had limited out on John Ringnecks at 3:30 p.m.

Following this, after Jan and Bob had downed another quail or two, we then went back to the vehicles, loaded up the dogs, making certain this time that all their door latches were well secured. Twenty minutes later found us parked around two old barns on a 200-acre place which Dick and I had hunted for years and which we were certain had an abundance of both quail and pheasants. Dick, Bob and I immediately began hunting around the barns since they were surrounded by about six acres of weeds and switch grass, ideal for our feathered friends.

Jan took two of his dogs and crossed a cornfield to hunt a draw which stretched out to another open field of lespedeza in the distance. Both he and Bob were intent on hunting quail; Bob, in particular, every year near the end of the fall and January hunting season, is almost a fanatic about pursuing them since he guides persons almost every day in southwest Iowa on pheasant hunts. In fact, he and my brother-in-law, Virgil Tagtmeyer, went up to Iowa on a one-day hunt on January 6, 2000. By 3:30 p.m. Virgil told me that they had five pheasants. Bob had bagged three, his daily limit, and Virgil had gotten two and was yearning for a good final shot at a rooster.

However, both Brie and Hazel, Bob's two pointers, froze on point in a hedge row, and when Bob and Virgil moved in, a big covey of bobwhites boomed out right under their feet. Each of them scored on a bird, and then Bob told Virgil, "I want to take home my limit in bobs, and I want to follow these birds up." Virgil said he groaned under his breath and muttered to himself, "Oh, God, there goes my chance of getting that last ringneck I need." Indeed, such proved to be the case, and he went home short one pheasant for himself on that hunt!

Back to our Kansas hunt several years ago. While searching the six acres of cover around the barns, it wasn't long until Bob's dogs whirled in and zeroed in on a large group of quail, and when he bumped them out, he racked one up. Dick and I now knew that we wouldn't get any help from either him or Jan for quite a while in searching for roosters since they both were engrossed in finding single birds from the coveys they had flushed. Up the draw where Jan had gone, we could hear some shooting. So we left Bob and crossed over to a shelter of thick cedar trees about a hundred and 25 yards in length out in a cornfield. We had experienced good luck there on ringnecks in the past.

While working these trees carefully, we heard Bob shoot a time or two, and when we were about 30 yards from the end of the grove, we heard another bang from Bob's over-and-under Browning Superposed 12-gauge, and then we heard him yell, "I missed him, and he's flying high, barreling your way!" I looked up over my head and, sure enough, a rooster was moving rapidly at least 45 to 55 yards up. I raised my A5 12-gauge Browning with its improved modified choke and cranked off a quick shot, not expecting to connect, but I was wrong.

The bird raised up in the air and then commenced falling, falling and hit down in the cornfield, but our vision of him was obstructed by the thick trees. I told Dick that we probably would never find him, but he thought differently and said, "He should be fairly easy to spot in the snow or to track if he wasn't dead when he hit the ground. Out in the cornfield, we cranked Zip up and encouraged her to hunt diligently for the bird, but in spite of an intensive search, she couldn't pin-point it. Then suddenly Dick exclaimed, "I believe I see him about 40 yards over to the left near that isolated corn stalk." Sure enough, when we walked over there, the ringneck was stone dead. It looked gorgeous in the snow with its strikingly beautiful colors and, of course, it was even more of a prize than usual because it filled out my limit for that memorable day.

Amazingly, when I checked my gun for the shells I was shooting at that time, there were quail loads in it instead of pheasant ones, because I had forgotten to change back to them after having hunted around the barns with Bob. This fact made my lucky long shot even more remarkable.

Dick and I sauntered back to the vehicles, and within a half hour, just before dark, Bob and Jan came in with their limit in quail and each had another pheasant which added to their take for the day. Needless to say, it took us over an hour to clean all of the game, which we always prefer to do in the field rather than at the motel because the motel game-cleaning room is always overcrowded and considerable waiting is involved. This delays our savoring a good hearty meal to satisfy our hunger as a result of all of the wholesome exercise connected with the hunt. In fact, that night meal with one's close hunting buddies is always one of the highlights of any hunt.

When six of us hunted out in Central Kansas the opening weekend in mid-November 1999, several years after the above described adventure, we encountered many, many more hunters than we ever had in the past, and we had been hunting virtually the same properties since 1962 (Dick since 1959). For example, when we six were ready to hunt 120 acres of prime switch grass which used to be private land but is now walk-in for anyone, 15 minutes before we were ready to commence driving through it on opening morning, six vehicles pulled up 50 yards from us and, believe it or not, 22 hunters from Colorado piled out with six dogs and completely dominated the heart of the field and swept it like a vacuum cleaner.

I counted the number of pheasants they killed — 37 — and only four escaped their hideous dragnet! Every time they downed a bird, they whooped and yelled and threw their hats up in the air, clapping their hands. Suffice it to say, none of us bagged any ringnecks from that field, but we did get eight over across the road on private land where the mob-army couldn't hunt.

Incredibly, later in the day, while we were hunting the 640 acres of land described in this story where I got that double on pheasants up the long winding draw, we looked behind us, and guess what! There those 22 men were following behind us about a quarter of a mile sweeping the place clean. We seriously doubt that they had permission to hunt there since the landowner is a prominent farmer and truck driver who is often away from home.

In my view, the Kansas Department of Wildlife & Parks should establish a rule that no more than eight or ten hunters can hunt public land or walk-in land at any one time. That way, the field would be much safer to hunt and an army of hunters would not hog or ruin other peoples' hunts and desecrate so many birds at once. The idea of walk-in land for hunters is excellent, for it helps those who are less able to get in on private land, but the privilege should not be abused. To prevent walk-in land hunting abuse, strict laws are necessary, or else Kansas will find itself in a few years much diminished in pheasant numbers and will experience a big loss in hunter revenue as has happened on several occasions in other states.

A HUNTER IS BORN

Richard Cooper, 1968

MY FRIEND, Don Lamm, allowed his older son, Art, to begin hunting with us in 1967. It began a lifelong love affair with the sport for Art which continues to this day. He devotes many days each fall to hunting pheasants, quail, Hungarian partridge, chukars and waterfowl in the area where he lives in eastern Oregon.

The next year younger son, Bob, joined us even though the Browning Sweet 16 which he shouldered was almost as large as he was. He soon learned to shoot it with credible accuracy, and he graduated to the level of sharpshooter on a memorable quail hunt near the little town of Smithton, Missouri, just four days before Christmas 1968.

It was a gray, winterish day with the temperature hovering just a degree or two above freezing. Occasional light rain fell, but never enough to interfere with our hunting.

We had two dogs with us. Mine was the first bird dog I ever owned, a beautifully proportioned female English setter I named Ginger. I had bought her from a barber in the small community of Iantha, Missouri, when she was less than a year old. After about another year, I put her with a trainer for three months, and she rounded into an outstanding dog.

I don't believe that registration papers make a great deal of difference in developing a good bird finder. More important is how the dog is trained and handled. I had put Ginger with a trainer I had known literally all of my life since he was the uncle of a childhood friend of mine. With three months training, I had an outstanding dog, one that was unwavering on point and soft-mouthed on retrieve.

The man I bought her from had registered her litter, so I followed through and acquired registration papers on her. This may

The day a real hunter was added to the ranks of the sport. Don, son Bob and myself after a fabulously successful quail hunt near Smithton, Missouri, December 21, 1968.

seem to contradict my earlier statement, but in a couple of years I ordered a pedigree from American Field more out of curiosity than anything else. Several generations back was the name Mississippi Zev, so she came from good blood lines if that's of any value.

On that chilly and damp day, both dogs turned in outstanding performances. They located four coveys, all of which held solidly until we kicked them out of the wet brush. Each had between 20 and 25 birds, and they held together after being flushed so that we had some excellent singles shooting. Adding frosting to the cake was the fact that nearly all of the shooting was in the open, unencumbered by trees or tall brush.

When we headed for home, we had 25 quail and a pre-teenager who had grown into a full-fledged bird hunter in one remarkable day's shooting.

Before we dressed the birds, I placed my old Sears 35 mm camera on a tripod and took a self-timed picture of the three of us in front of the fireplace in Don's family room with all 25 birds spread out between us. The tassel-headed kid grinning in the picture is now a bearded 40-something professional fishing guide in Idaho who comes back to Missouri each fall and occasionally lets us two old crocks hunt with him so that he can show us how the sport should really be done.

THOSE BUZZING BOBS ...
WHAT A GREAT DAY!

Don Lamm, 1988

IT WAS A WARM late November day in 1988 when my son-in-law, David Gail, and I headed out for a couple of farms near Hughesville, 12 miles north of Sedalia, Missouri, for a good time with the four to five coveys of bobwhites which we knew were there.

Accompanying us were David's two Brittanies, Paddy and J.R., Paddy being four years of age and an experienced and proven bird finder, and J.R. being 15 months, but having participated on a number of hunts. My brown and white eight-year-old setter, Flair, and Brownie, my black and white 18-month-old English setter, filled out the hunting party.

Twenty minutes or so away from David's truck, Paddy came down on a rock solid point, and Brownie, the best bird dog I ever owned, immediately backed. At least 20 to 25 buzzing bobs burst out of the weeds in all directions, with at least 10 of them flying ahead of us into a clump of trees about 125 yards away.

On the covey rise just described, David's A500 12-gauge Browning semi-automatic downed two birds, and my A5 Browning 12 semi-auto dropped one. Paddy retrieved the two bobs David shot back to him, and Flair brought the one I got halfway back to me.

Upon approaching the birds which had settled into the trees, Flair ran up ahead of us and flushed them prematurely and, of course, David and I both were quite unhappy about that. However, five minutes later, we noticed that Paddy and J.R. were both birdy, as was Brownie. Flair was off somewhere else on her own.

This time, Brownie made the point and Paddy and J.R. backed beautifully, like statues. Two birds buzzed noisily out of the grassy knoll, and David bagged his third of the day. I missed. We then walked a quarter of a mile where we were certain another group of birds resided, but Flair got there first, and she bumped them out well ahead of us, denying us a chance to shoot. As described in one of my stories in this book, "Bird Dogs I've Had Over The Past 60 Years," I emphasized the fact that Flair was an outstanding dove hunting dog and good at finding and pointing single quail, but most of her covey finds were disasters because she wouldn't hold.

Her flushing of the group of birds, described above, annoyed both David and I to no end, and I ran up to Flair, snapped a rope to her collar and tied her up to a tree, where she lay down. We then resumed our hunt toward the place where the bulk of the bobs went that Flair had bumped.

The quail had strung out over a 60 or 70-yard stretch of fox grass which was 25 feet wide and bordered a cornfield on one side and some persimmon trees and sumac on the other. When she came to the fox grass, Paddy halted into a marble-like stance, backed by Brownie with J.R. eight feet behind, frozen, too. The bird flew behind me upon flushing, and it bit the dust 30 yards out, my second one of the day. After depositing it in my hunting coat, we walked forward 20 or 30 paces, and Brownie stopped, looking intently right down at her feet. The other two dogs honored her point. Two birds burst forth and we were ready. David racked up number four, and I put number three in the bag.

Believe it or not, we got five more superb points in that fox grass, and David and I each nailed two more birds apiece, making a total of six for David and five for me. Lunchtime coaxed us back to David's truck, where we unloaded the game and deposited Flair into her portable kennel for the remainder of the day.

An hour later we started to hunt the second adjoining farm which we had permission to hunt, and during the afternoon we witnessed some fantastic dog work in every respect, location of the birds, magnificent points, finding of dead birds and exceptional retrieves, especially by Paddy. One particular event which I vividly recall was when David dropped the leg on a quail which had been pointed by J.R. It flew 75 yards up a draw, and when we arrived at the place where we thought it went down, all three dogs searched diligently for 10 minutes with no results. Finally, we saw J.R. 25 yards away on a firm point, and when we walked right up to her, she jumped in and came up with the bird in her mouth and gave it to David.

Happy we were at near day's end when we headed home, each

with our limit of 10 mature bobs. Even more satisfying were the two delicious Sunday dinners we had; one at David's house, when his lovely wife, Cindy, did the honors, and the other when my beautiful spouse, Connie, did the same.

I have been the photographer on a majority of our hunting trips. This is probably the best quail hunting action shot I ever took. Bill Glenn and Don level off on a covey rise of 14 birds (count 'em) on Bill's 320-acre farm in Pettis County, Missouri, January 11, 1975.

WHEN THE SHOOTING GETS
HOT AND HEAVY

Richard Cooper, 1976

THERE IS NO BETTER WAY to end a quail season than the way that Bob Lamm and I did in early January of 1976. It was a clear and crisp Sunday afternoon, and the season closed in just four days. Consequently, it was our last effort until the season reopened 10 months later.

We had planned to make it a threesome, but Bob's father, Don, pulled out when a trace of snow and ice had failed to melt as expected. He had severely strained the muscles in his right leg the season before when he stepped into an unexpectedly soft area of sand and mud along a creek bank. The possibility of reinjury on any kind of a slick surface created a risk which he was unwilling to take.

We headed out to a farm northwest of Sedalia where we had found birds the previous season but had not visited during the current season. An hour spent behind my setter, Jack, and Don's setter, Dana, a littermate, produced a large covey and some good shooting. We bagged about five bobwhites between us.

From there, we moved a short distance up the road to another farm where we had found a couple of coveys the previous year. We started up a short but dense hedgerow, the type of Osage Orange trees which are few in number in these days of virtual fence to fence tilling and planting. We had not gone far before both dogs began to creep, sure fire evidence that they were trailing a covey. The slow creeping continued to the point where the hedgerow dead ended in a deep fescue field. The stealthy pursuit continued about 15 yards out into the field, at which point both dogs settled into solid points. However, neither dog was honoring the other; each was pointing a bird, or birds, out of the line of vision of the other. We approached Jack first, and one bird roared into the air. I downed it at about 25 yards, and Jack pranced ahead to make the retrieve. After putting it in the bag, we headed over to Dana, but before we got to her two more birds were in the air. Bob downed one, and Dana's bird had had enough as it, too, flushed. Jack dashed out to retrieve Bob's bird since it fell closer to him, and he had no sooner started back with it than he halted in midstride, pointing still another bird.

I'll never understand how a dog's olfactory system works. Carrying a bird just under its nose and identifying the scent of another bird on the ground at the same time seems impossible, but I know that it has happened many times. This was my first time to witness it.

The next few minutes were filled with whirring wings, dogs on point, dogs retrieving and the pungent smell of smokeless powder. Since both of us were carrying two-barrels, Bob with an over-and-under and me with a side-by-side, there were several fumbling visits to our shell vests to reload. Finally I realized that if my hurried mental count was accurate, we were approaching our limits, which in 1975-76 in Missouri was eight birds. I shouted the wild melee to a halt, and we began to count birds. Bob had his limit, and I had seven. Since Dana was on point again, I walked ahead to her and quickly harvested my eighth bird.

Before we could go back to the truck, we had to pull the dogs off of still more points. I'll never know how many birds there were in that covey, but it must have been 25 to 30. Obviously they had run ahead of us out into the fescue and squatted under the dense grass hoping to elude us. Thanks to the keen noses of two great dogs, we had a few minutes of the wildest quail shooting which it is possible to have. I doubt that either of us will ever experience such happy madness again, and we still left nearly 20 birds behind.

THE INVISIBLE QUAIL, OR WAS IT?

Don Lamm, 1972

ONE OF MY MOST FOND MEMORIES during over a half century of avidly hunting Mr. Bobwhite in west central Missouri was the time when my affectionate but deadly efficient little brown and white setter, Jaynee, came down on point solidly , as she always did. Indeed, she was a "natural," and seldom if ever made a faux paux.

Being by myself on a Tuesday, which was one of my two "off" days as a college instructor since I taught long hours including night classes the other three days of the week, I took three steps forward … and 24 to 28 bombshells exploded right in front of me. Leveling off my A-5 semi-automatic Browning 12-gauge with its poly choke, I picked my birds individually and got off three shots in rapid order.

To my astonishment, four quail dropped, and within minutes three of them were in the bag, but the evasive number four bob simply could not be found, even though Jaynee and I spent a full 20 minutes combing every inch of what I thought was an adequate area. In fact, after such a concentrated effort, I began to think, "Did I really drop that fourth bird?" Did I see an invisible quail?

I then abandoned the search and went on to hunt the remainder of the farm, got superb points with two other coveys and by 2:15 p.m. had nine birds in my hunting coat, just one short of my limit.

Then my mind returned to that lost fourth bird, and I just knew for certain that I had knocked it down, and it just had to be there. I remembered an article about bird hunting which I had read two weeks previously in an outdoor magazine in which the author had stressed, "When a wounded or downed bird cannot be found, leave the search and then return later in the day, or even the next day in case of pheasants, and have your dog or dogs search carefully for it again."

So, that's exactly what I did. I said to myself, "I know that I can easily get another bird to fill out my limit, but I want my number ten bob to be the wounded one I knocked down several hours ago. To me, one wounded bird in the bag is worth two in the bush. Upon reapproaching the grassy area and clump of trees where the big bunch had roared out of that morning, sure enough, within three minutes little Jaynee (only slightly over half as large as a normal female setter, but very strong) locked in solid again. Readying my gun for a fast flyout, no such thing occurred, and the dog then poked her nose into a heavy tuft of grass and came up with the dropped legged quail in its mouth. Needless to say, I arrived home in the middle of the afternoon on that beautiful late fall day a happy hunter.

The moral of this story is that when a bird is wounded, knocked down and can't be found, it often holes up in heavy cover or runs a considerable distance and for some reason gives off very little, if any, scent and thus can't be located by the dogs. Often hunters don't let their dogs range out far enough in their search for either wounded quail or pheasants, and they keep too close a rein on their dogs. In regard to ringnecks, my present female setter, Zipper, has found wounded ones three to four blocks from the place they were shot down. On several occasions she has located wounded birds the next day.

Anyway, if the hunter returns several hours later the same day on quail and even the next day on pheasants, there is a good chance of bagging the bird with no extra expense of a shotgun shell or two, and the dog will experience an extra thrill finding and retrieving the bird while gaining valuable experience.

HISTORICAL EVENT COINCIDED WITH A QUAIL HUNT

Richard Cooper, 1963

THIS IS NOT just an account of a quail hunt, be it successful or unsuccessful. The fact that a quail hunt was involved in the story is only a coincidence, an attendant activity which occurred on a date on which an already stunned America would undergo still another body blow to its psyche.

The date was November 24, 1963. For many readers, the event to which I have referred is already apparent.

For the sake of the telling, permit me to develop the story.

It was two days after the assassination of John F. Kennedy. The American people had recoiled in horror at the event in Dallas and had collectively settled back to digest what had happened. A pall of national mourning seemed to spread across the country. Virtually all events, public and private, had been cancelled in the aftermath with the exception of the Oklahoma-Nebraska football game which was played anyway despite an outpouring of public disapproval.

I was home with my wife ruminating on the event of just 48 hours prior, like most everyone else. It was just the second year of my 30-year teaching career at Smith-Cotton High School in Sedalia, Missouri.

Then it became apparent to me that being cloistered at home didn't contribute anything useful to the national condition. I called a friend, Walt Diehl, and conveyed the same outlook to him, suggesting that it certainly wouldn't harm anything if we went bird hunting for two or three hours. He was in full agreement.

Walt was the vice-principal at Smith-Cotton and was also in his second year at the school. He was a native Kansan and had a love for the quail bird equal to mine.

I loaded my setter into the trunk of my car, drove by and picked up Walt and headed for a mutual friend's farm which had proven to be a bird producer just a week before. The farm was located about 14 miles north of Sedalia near the small community of Hughesville.

Bob Smith raised hogs and also had several fields of row crops. He had left plenty of brush between fields and along his border fences, knowing the needs of quail and other wildlife. He also was an avid quail hunter, having gone with us a couple of times already that season.

We stopped at the house fully expecting Bob to go with us, but he declined saying that he had several projects which had to be completed, including some plumbing repair inside the house. He told us to have a good hunt, and he would catch us next time.

After exchanging a few more pleasantries, we headed out through the barn lot into some of the finest quail cover to be found in Pettis County.

It was a rather windy afternoon and unseasonably warm. It must have been at least 70 degrees, and even shell vests made us uncomfortably warm.

We found plenty of birds, and each of us got four or five apiece in the brief time we had to hunt. The most memorable incident involved my setter, Ginger. She was my first bird dog and one of my best, always solid on point and readily honoring other dogs who had found birds. In fact, on a number of occasions she had frozen to honor fertilizer sacks and other light-colored objects in fields until finally realizing that they were not other dogs on point. One of her strongest attributes was retrieving, always seeking out downed birds and bringing them back to me and holding them lightly in her mouth until I gave the command, "Give." She had been force-broken to retrieve by H. F. Lane, a nationally known trainer near my little hometown of Liberal in southwest Missouri. In fact, as this is being written, Mr. Lane is preparing to celebrate his 100th birthday.

When Ginger retrieved a bird, she would bring it only to me, no matter who downed it. Of course, this was as it should be, but when she was prevented from doing so on that warm and windy November afternoon, a humorous and somewhat frustrating incident occurred.

Walt and I were walking on opposites of a deep brushy draw. Ginger pointed a scattered single on Walt's side, and he downed it easily at 30 to 35 yards. She bounded out for the downed bird and quickly found it. However, at that point, she saw that she was not going to be able to bring the bird to me since the draw, more like a ravine, was virtually impenetrable. As the frustrated dog stood with the bird held gently in her mouth, I called to Walt and told him the best course of action would be to lower his hand and gently say "Give." Unfortunately, Ginger would have none of it, and as Walt approached she consumed the bird, feathers, feet and all. To this day, I can still hear Walt's anguished cry, "She ate my bird."

Shortly afterwards, we headed to the house for another short visit with Bob and then the trip home. As we retraced our steps of less than three hours before, we saw Bob come out of the back door with a strange expression on his face. As we approached him, he seemed to sputter as he blurted out, "Just awhile ago, I saw the damnedest thing I ever saw in my life. I saw a man murdered on television."

Of course, what he had seen was the live television coverage of Jack Ruby's murder of Lee Harvey Oswald in the basement of the Dallas, Texas police station. Indeed, it was the nation's first live televised murder.

Our trip back to Sedalia that late afternoon was a quiet one, filled with more ruminating on the events in Dallas which had stunned the nation.

FAREWELL, QUAIL HEAVEN

Richard Cooper, 1975

ALL OF US who have hunted upland game have our favorite spots, places we would prefer to hunt more than any other. Usually, they are places where we have experienced our most consistent success, although other factors may also contribute to our warm feeling, factors such as the lay of the land or the people who live there.

For Don Lamm, Bill Glenn and me, the favorite of favorites was a small farm located far back in the brush of eastern Pettis County, Missouri. Its total area was less than 100 acres, and it belonged to a grizzled old farmer named Hubert Finley.

Hubert was the antithesis of the efficient and progressive farmer. His farming practices were as far as it's possible to get from those of a successful farmer. He would plant 15 acres of milo and harvest only seven or eight. His fences were in wretched condition, filled with undergrowth so thick that it was extremely difficult to get over them. Some of the barbed wire would probably have qualified for an agricultural museum.

A wind storm blew over a large elm tree in his front yard, alarmingly close to his house. Five years later the tree was still there, reduced in size somewhat as Hubert had cut the smaller limbs for firewood.

His barn lot was a graveyard of old tractors and pieces of machinery, most of which had rusted into a solid piece of oxidized metal. Some of the old tractors dated back to the early 1930s.

This near total neglect of the place created an ideal environment for quail. You couldn't have designed a more perfect haven for bobwhites.

Hubert's income from farming must have been extremely small. The family breadwinner was his hard-working wife, Adelaide, who taught school in the nearby community of Smithton. She was a respected member of the school's faculty, and a room at the high school is named in her honor.

Hubert was reluctant to allow anyone to hunt on his place, but Don had known him for many years. The fact that Don was allowed to hunt rabbits there as a young boy led to the granting of permission to hunt as an adult. He was allowed to bring his two friends with him, and consequently we had the place to ourselves. A hunt at Hubert Finley's was always a treat, but there was a certain ritual which had to be followed. Before hunting, we always had to sit down and visit for at least 30 minutes. The subject may have been grain prices, the seeing of wild game, or just the weather. Serious or frivolous, the visit was a requirement.

Each Christmas we would take a five-pound box of chocolates out to them as a gesture of appreciation for their hospitality.

Shortly after Mrs. Finley retired from her long teaching career, Hubert suffered a fatal heart attack. Soon after that, she moved into Sedalia and within a few months had sold the farm to a local doctor who owned an adjoining farm. He intended to combine it with his farm after removing the brush.

We secured permission to hunt the place one last time on December 20, 1975. The entry in my hunting diary speaks for itself. "Hunted Hubert Finley farm during the morning, finding only one bird. West side bulldozed clean, and much of north side also gone. Sad! Sad!"

We continued taking the box of Christmas chocolates to Mrs. Finley until her death about four years later.

Today, that land is farmed from fence post to fence post. It is kept so clean of brush that a field mouse could hardly find living space ... and many wonder where all the quail have gone.

Section 3
WATERFOWL

THREE DOWN IN QUICK ORDER

Don Lamm, 1944 and 1957

Nineteen Fifty-Seven proved to be one of the most exciting years of my life as far as hunting was concerned. By the end of October, I had shot over 200 doves and a good many pigeons and was thus sharpened up for the bobwhites and any waterfowl that I might chance to encounter while on an outing. I had not yet gotten into any kind of serious waterfowl hunting as was to be the case six to seven years later as described in several of my other stories in this book.

A thrilling isolated event concerning waterfowl had occurred a number of years before in the fall of 1944, after I had graduated from high school, but before I got into World War II. I was working for my father and uncle on their 1100-acre farm just west of Sedalia, Missouri, and was picking ears of corn, throwing them into a wagon pulled by a team of mules.

About 4 p.m. I started in toward the barn to end my day's work, and in the big field where I was working there was a large pond where I had seen waterfowl before, but another man and his wife had permission to hunt it and I never was there at the right time.

However, as my empty wagon rumbled out of the field, I glanced over to the pond some 60 to 70 yards away, and there they were, some eight or nine nice-sized Canada geese sitting on it, completely at ease. Upon seeing this, I speeded up the mules, reached the barn, hastily unharnessed and fed them, jumped into my father's car and sped into town three miles away. I then got my 16-gauge Ithaca featherweight pump gun out of the closet at my parent's house and grabbed up some shells.

Upon passing the pond 20 minutes earlier, I had noticed that the honkers were out in the pond about 20 to 25 yards from its north bank, which was high. Thus, a perfect set-up for a sneak was plainly in evidence. When I topped the bank, the geese immediately saw me and flushed noisily. I got off three rapid shots, and two of them lay threshing on the surface of the water while the others lumbered away yelping. Indeed, I was a happy 18-year-old lad that night as I plucked them for the family's upcoming Thanksgiving dinner.

Back to 1957. On a late fall Saturday morning about 10 a.m., I was out hunting quail by myself in that same field with my cousin Beasmore Lamm's liver and white pointer, Rex. I had hunted with this dog two or three times previously, and he really was an industrious bird finder and had a stylish point. It was a privilege to hunt with him, and Bease was always amenable to my using him whenever I wished.

As we began going down a long rather broad draw where I had shot many a bobwhite before, both by myself and with Bill Glenn, about one-third of the way through it, without finding any quail, I decided I'd better check that pond for any ducks or geese. I held my breath, hoping I could keep the dog in check so as to prevent him from reaching the pond too far ahead of me and flushing up anything that might be on it.

Well, attempts to rein the dog in quietly were unsuccessful, and Rex barreled up toward the pond with me well behind. No chance for a surprise sneak up the bank here! Fortunately, Rex hustled clear around the steep pond bank and went over to the far side of the pond. When that happened, pandemonium broke loose, and at least 20 mallards got up, and not seeing me 25 yards from the pond, they flew right over me, several of them low. I raised my old reliable ll-48 Remington 12-gauge semi-automatic and, carefully picking my birds, I squeezed off three rounds. To my surprise, three tumbled to the ground, seemingly quite close together.

I ran over and picked up two dead drakes instantly, but I didn't see the third duck. A search began which lasted for a full 15 minutes, and I finally found the wounded hen 25 yards from where she had hit the ground, crouched down in some thick weeds. I was elated about finding her, and after putting the three ducks in my hunting coat's game bag, Rex and I proceeded on down the draw. He soon locked up on a nice covey of quail, and within 20 minutes I added three bobs to the pot. I then headed home with a total of three plus three equals six, a more than ample take on a half-day's outing.

Don Lamm with the three mallard ducks he bagged in 1957. Four-year-old son, Art, shared in the enthusiasm of the moment.

Needless to say, when I did arrive home, my four-year-old son, Art, was at the door eagerly awaiting my return, ready to help me clean the game, before which the above picture was taken.

BOB'S FIRST GOOSE

Don Lamm, 1968

IN THE FALL OF 1968, when my younger son, Bob, was 12 years old, I decided to take him on his first honker hunt. At that time I belonged to a goose club not far from the big Swan Lake Federal Wildlife Reservation in Chariton County, Missouri. The club was known as the Santa Fe Club, since the Santa Fe Railroad adjoined its south side. Some 15 of us belonged, and we would get into blinds on the edge of fields and into a wooded draw which wound its way through the middle of its 200 acres. The land was owned by Rush Johnson, vice president in charge of sales for Walsworth Publishing Company of Marceline, Missouri, at the time, and he was also a prominent farmer in the area. Rush had a house on the property which he encouraged the club members to use, and we had many hours of good fellowship which included fish and steak fries and card games.

On this particular day, Bob and I got into one of the blinds at daybreak, but by 9 a.m. we had not gotten a shot. We went back to the house for some coffee and a snack. Then, upon looking across the road north of the house, we noticed that the hunters in two of the blinds were getting geese. When they filled out with their one honker each, we walked over and asked them if we could get in their blinds, and they gave us the green light.

Bob seated himself into one blind and I got into the other. Since he had never shot a honker, I gave him some advice about leading the birds, letting them get close, and so forth, which I thought might help. For three years previously he had gone quail hunting with me and had bagged a considerable number of bobwhites, so he had some rudimentary knowledge of shooting and hunting.

Not long after crawling into those above ground circular grass-covered blinds, a big goose swung in close to Bob, and he shot twice with his 12-gauge A5 semi automatic Browning and missed. A half-hour later a nice honker flew over my blind and I nailed it. I then got into the blind with Bob, and in the space of an hour or so he got two more close shots, but still didn't connect. After that, nothing more occurred, and later in the day two different members of that club returned, and we had to get out and go to our own club. Back at the Santa Fe Club, we got zero shots late that afternoon.

Twelve-year-old Bob Lamm bagged this 12-pound Canada goose, left, near Swan Lake, Missouri, on October 27, 1968. The seven-pounder on the right was bagged by his father on the same day.

We remained the night at the club house and awoke early the next morning to a chilly, windy, blustery day. We went out to a Santa Fe Club blind, got a long shot at a Canada flying up the draw, but drew a blank. About 10 a.m. we went across the road and got into the same two blinds described above, but by 11:30 neither of us had gotten a shot. I was getting quite cold, so I told Bob I was going back to the house. He said, "Dad, I've been observing some geese flying over the levy about a half mile away, and I'm going to see if I can score on a goose." I remarked, "Good luck, I'll be waiting."

An hour passed, and as I looked out the window of the Santa Fe Club house, across the road I saw my son about 125 yards away approaching with a really large goose extending down from his right arm almost dragging the ground. When he arrived, we admired the goose, I congratulated Bob, and then weighed his prize which came to exactly 12 pounds, a pound for each year Bob happened to be. After that day his shooting of geese improved markedly until some 20 years later he was besting me in both weight and numbers almost every year.

What a delight!

Today, at age 43 he professionally guides waterfowlers during the month of October in the western part of the United States. From mid-May to October 1, he guides trout fishermen down the Henry's Fork of the Snake, the Madison and the Gallatin rivers, and for the remainder of the year he trains retrieving dogs.

To be learned from this story is that a father who has sons and/or daughters should take an avid interest in their well-being and do things with them that are interesting and exciting. Teaching youth to hunt and to experience with them the out-of-doors is one of the best ways to do this. During my early teen

One hog of a rainbow trout caught in 1971 at Bennett Springs, Missouri, by 15-year-old Bob Lamm. The lunker weighed 14 pounds, 6 ounches, and held the state record for over three years.

age years back in the early 1940s, my father and my uncle owned an 1100-acre farm immediately west of the Missouri State Fair grounds near Sedalia, Missouri. These two wise men built a cabin for me and my first cousin, Henry Lamm, with some lumber left over from a house my father had torn down in town.

For several years, I took several of my close friends out to that cabin and we hunted quail and rabbits, some of which we cleaned and cooked over the open fire place. The weekends we spent there went a long way toward shaping our behavior in a favorable and constructive way and promoting wholesome fellowship.

Even prior to our years spent in the cabin, Bill Glenn, a life-long friend of mine, and I used to walk from town out to my father and uncle's farm and roam all over it as 11 and 12-year-olders hunting mostly rabbits, but also shooting at whatever quail we might encounter. We had no hunting dogs that early in our lives; they were to come later. Anyway, on an average day spent hunting that farm in those days, we bagged somewhere between four and eight rabbits each and perhaps one to three quail.

At day's end, we would trudge, dead tired, back to my father and mother's house, and my dear, sweet mother and understanding father would allow us to clean all of our game in the kitchen, which shielded us from the cold that was sometimes intense. The odor was horrific, especially when we opened up the rabbits, and how my parents were able to endure this activity, both Bill and I have pondered to this very day. Very few parents would ever have tolerated it. So I was indeed most fortunate to have loving parents who were interested beyond the call of duty in their son's activities and those of his friends.

When my own two sons came along a generation later and were old enough to hunt at ages 10 to 12 years, I began taking them dove, quail, rabbit and waterfowl hunting, and the payoff has been that my sons today are avid outdoorsmen and haven't gotten into trouble like a good many young men who have no fathers around or have fathers who show no interest in what they do.

My older son, Donald Arthur Lamm, age 47, and I have hunted together for years, and every spring and fall he flies in from the west and we turkey hunt near Sedalia. He usually always gets his two gobblers each time he comes, and he has a lot of good places to hunt. We also have had many enjoyable honker and duck hunts at Turkey Creek farm. This past fall he gave me a free plane ticket on Southwest Airline, and I spent five fantastic days with him and his wife in Adrian, Oregon, which is a small town on the Snake River very close to the Idaho border. He and I hunted pheasants, ducks, chukars, huns and quail and had a great time. He got most of the birds, but I derived a great deal of satisfaction knowing that I had much to do with teaching him how to hunt and shoot.

Time invested in one's sons or daughters early in their lives nearly always pays big dividends.

A LONG DAY IN THE GOOSE PITS

Don Lamm, Late 1960s

FOR WELL OVER 30 YEARS I was part owner of a 132-acre private goose and duck hunting club adjacent to the huge federal Swan Lake Wildlife Reservation in Chariton County Missouri. In its prime years from the 1940s through the 1980s as many as 200,000 Canadian geese, 60,000 blues and snows, 50,000 to 60,000 ducks taking into account the adjoining Fountain Grove Reservation, plus a multitude of deer, some trophy specimens, wintered there. Obviously, the creation of this hunter's paradise in 1934 under the first administration of Franklin D. Roosevelt provided superb thrills and adventures for hunters for decades, and it still does.

Since I have never gotten into deer hunting, either by bow or gun, my principal reason for "investing" thousands of dollars into this waterfowl club enterprise was the fact that as an instructor of economics and psychology at a community college at Sedalia, Missouri, I taught a heavy day and night course load three days a week and had all day Tuesday and Thursday off, which allowed me to hunt four full days a week, counting weekends. Also, I had two teenage sons who loved to hunt waterfowl and upland game birds, so my money spent as part owner of this club was certainly not completely wasted. In addition, my own father, a prominent Sedalia, Missouri attorney for over 60 years, said to me one day, "Son, a young man who is encouraged to hunt by his father will usually always stay out of trouble." Over the years, such has proven to be the case. Both of my sons, now in their mid-40s, are avid hunters and fishermen, and one of them is a professional fishing and waterfowl guide in Idaho and also trains retrieving dogs.

With all of the above as an introduction, of the many memories which I carry with me in regard to my honker hunts at Turkey Creek Farm, Inc., the name of the club, the long, long day in the goose pits

Six-year-old daughter, Carrie, admires a large Canada taken by Don Lamm early one morning at Turkey Creek Farm in 1984.

stands out as being the most vivid. The hunting at the club from the 1940s through the 1980s was so good that one could usually get in the blind and within an hour or two have several ducks in the bag plus one or two Canada geese, whatever was allowed at the time, which fluctuated throughout the season at the whims of the federal game regulators. Occasionally, opportunities presented themselves, too, for a blue, snow or whitefront goose, but the Canadas were far more numerous and much easier to get. Also they were usually the better prize because of their larger size.

In the mornings when the shooting started, the roar of the guns both on the reservation and on all of the private clubs surrounding it sounded almost like the Western Front in World War I, the activity was that intense! One morning at a club across the road from ours, called Cuddy's, 14 hunters walked in at daylight and got into three large blinds. An hour and a half later all 14 of them walked back out, each with his honker.

Well, on this particular morning of the long, long day, I plopped myself into one of the better blinds at Turkey Creek down by the levy close to the reservation, all ready to go. Within 25 minutes after shooting began, two Canadas cruised over the blind at about 45 yards, and I led the first one 10 to 15 yards and cranked off a shot at it with my full choke A5 Browning 12-gauge semi-automatic, but nothing happened! I was shocked since I had been shooting quite well in recent days. Another shot at the other Canada also failed to connect.

Thirty minutes later at about 7:45 a.m., another honker presented itself as an ideal side shot at about 40 yards. Mentally, I said to myself, "He's in the skillet; the family will have a savory goose on the table for Sunday dinner." The gun barked once, no kill; twice, no results; with no chance for a third try.

By this time, a couple of my friends were beginning to jeer at me, and inwardly I was furious at myself. I muttered, "The next one that comes over will be knocked silly, stone dead." At ten o'clock the next Canada did fly over sufficiently low for a perfect shot, but stone dead it did not become because I missed it clean, and I then heard one of the club members in another blind mumble in foul language loud enough for me to hear, "God —— I wish I were as lucky as he to get all those choice opportunities. I sure as h—— wouldn't blow my shots like he's been doing this morning."

Following that remark, I decided to leave Turkey Creek and go over to another goose club I belonged to adjacent to the reservation on its west side called the Tri County Sure Shots where I had scored on a number of geese on past occasions. When I got there, I received a warm welcome from the members who were there, all of whom had gotten their geese, and then they asked me if I had gotten mine yet. I told them part of my sad story, omitting some of the embarrassing details, and they then said, "We have great news for you. You know that small pond down there in the timber about three blocks away? Well, there are 10 or 12 Canadas which we just saw set in there 15 minutes ago, and if you sneak the bank of the pond very discreetly, you should get one." I exclaimed, "Man, that's great, I'll give it the old college try."

Upon peeking over the pond bank with the greatest of care not to be seen, the birds were there, close. I said to myself, "I don't want to shoot one on the water — that's unsportsmans-like, so I'll top the bank and nail one when they flush up. They're so close anyway, I can't miss!"

The A5 barked once. No honker fell, but feathers floated everywhere over the water. POW! Another shot at the geese farther away, but still well within killing range, failed to get the cherished reward. As the lucky gallant 12 winged their way back into the reservation, I trudged up the hill to my buddies and took my ribbings and queer looks from the club members because they had all witnessed with great interest the spectacle, fully expecting me to bring some meat back to camp. By this time, my shooting slump had truly become a curse.

Two o'clock in the afternoon found me back at Turkey Creek in a different blind down at the levy. I was now the only club member there, since the others had long since gotten their geese and had departed. At least now, I thought, no one is around to witness a disgraceful exhibition by me similar to those manifested all day up to that time.

A cold, hard rain began to fall, and I closed both blind doors, saying, "I'll never get a chance now because nothing will be flying in such miserable weather, but I'll stay in the blind hoping that the downpour will eventually let up." I also thought and even voiced out loud, "God, please let me get a goose today. I've gotten one every time I've been up here this year, and I don't want to have to drive 80 miles back to Sedalia empty-handed."

Well, the rain let up some, but not enough to open the blind doors. Nevertheless, 25 minutes after my little appeal to the Lord, I heard a loud honk right over the blind, and when I flipped open the doors in great haste, an eight-pound Canada was only 15 yards immediately above me. What a delightful surprise! I steadied up and got off what I thought were two perfect shots. But do you think the goose bit the mud as I anticipated? No, my prayer went unanswered, and I must confess that by this time I was completely frustrated and livid with anger. In all of my 35 years of hunting up to that time I had never experienced such humiliation and deprivation.

Resolving not to leave Turkey Creek until closing time, I remained in the blind another two hours. It came down to five minutes before time to cease shooting. Complete silence. No geese anywhere. Then, all of sudden, just two minutes before time to quit and get out of the blind, I heard one lone goose, albeit a small one flying quite high, yelping and headed for the reservation to joins its friends for the night. It came directly over the blind and was at least 60 yards up. Normally I never would have shot in such a scenario, but anger, anxiety and frustration told me, "It's now or never, nothing ventured, nothing gained," and shoot I did. What an incredibly beautiful sight, watching that long-necked five-pound Canada tumble from so far up and hit the ground within 20 yards of the blind.

That particular year, believe it or not, I bagged a honker at Turkey Creek every single time I went up, had no more horrible shooting slumps similar to those described above, and got 28 geese, one more than my son, Bob, who had said before the season opened, "This is the year I'm going to beat you, Dad." But he didn't, and several years transpired before he finally did.

What is to be gleaned from all of this? When one finds himself into a detestable shooting slump, whether for one day or several, changing guns often helps. I should have changed guns by mid-morning when I left Turkey Creek to go over to the Tri County Sure Shots Club, but I had such undaunted faith in my "Old Reliable" A5 that I couldn't separate myself from it, even temporarily.

I remember many years ago when I was out near Russell, Kansas, on a pheasant hunt with two other good friends. One of them, who was a crack shot, always used an old J.C. Higgins 12-gauge pump gun purchased at Sears Roebuck for a very minimal amount at the time ($49). He seldom missed, no matter how difficult the shot. On this particular day, though, I noticed he had a new 12-gauge pump of a different brand, and he proudly displayed it to us, saying his other gun was getting too beat up and he was tired of it.

Some 15 minutes later, a big ringneck got right up in front of his feet and flew straight away. POW! Missed. POW! Missed again. Then another rooster flushed just as close to him as the first one and he missed twice again. In a rage, he threw his gun down hard on the ground, as an angry golfer might do with one of his clubs, stomped on it, picked it up and dragged it back to his car and threw it into the trunk. Then he deftly shouldered his Higgins "Old Faithful" and within an hour and a half had his limit of four pheasants plus three extra bobwhites. He ended up his hunting career just a few years ago and at the time was still using only his old Higgins. Of course, in his case, anything other than that firearm was always a disaster. After that day of blowing it on those two roosters, he never shot any other gun. This is a case where using the same old gun proved to be best for him, whereas often for other hunters switching from one gun to another works out best.

Concerning my waterfowl hunting after the long, long day, I soon purchased an Ithaca 10-gauge and used it for geese, while also taking the A5 with me to the blind to use for ducks only. This helped a lot. In later years, I also purchased a 12-gauge Benelli which shoots shells in length from two and a half to three and a half inches. The three-and-a-half-inch 12-gauge shell almost matches a 10-gauge three-and-a-half-inch shell in killing power, and the 12-gauge gun is much lighter than the 10. The 12-gauge with the long shell makes an ideal goose and turkey gun, especially for a senior citizen.

The next lesson to be learned is that of unmitigated patience and persistence which applies to all kinds of hunting. Every good hunter knows this and makes it a cardinal rule on all of his or her outings. "One must hang in there" through thick or thin in all kinds of weather and in all kinds of psychologic setbacks of whatever nature. By my staying in the blind until the very end of the day, I achieved a payoff which would not have occurred had I abandoned the hunt in the early or mid afternoon. Psychologically, bagging a honker that day, even though it was a small one, and even though it was a long, long day in the blinds, helped my morale tremendously and enabled me to break the back of the shooting slump.

It was a great late afternoon of honker hunting in November 1979, at Turkey Creek Farm in Chariton County, Missouri. Left to right are Jack Williams, Greg Bell, Paul Nieder, Larry Ament, Don Lamm and Don's wife Connie.

SHOOT, WOMAN, SHOOT!

Don Lamm, 1980

SHORTLY AFTER I married my wife, Connie, 23 years ago, she and I went goose hunting at Turkey Creek Farm, Inc., a private property waterfowl club consisting of 132 acres of which I was part owner, located adjacent to the big Swan Lake Federal Wildlife Reservation in Chariton County, Missouri. At that time the honker hunting was exceptionally good, and nearly every hunter could get his or her goose plus some ducks as well within an hour or two.

Since Connie and I owned 40 percent of the club and there were ten blinds on the place, every time I went up my blind rotation permitted me four blinds to occupy, so with four persons allowed per blind, a good many of our close friends, mostly college instructor colleagues, came along, although we would allow only two persons per blind instead of four. Two of our friends, Greg and Karen Bell, also had a farm house two miles west of Triplett, Missouri, where we often stayed overnight, had steak fries and played cards.

Shooting time found Connie and me in a good blind down on the levy closest to the reservation where the honkers often came out low and at times circled around the decoys at heights of 10 to 12 feet within 20 to 35 yards of the blind. Several of our friends, all men, were in the other three pits. We thus had nearly all of the levy blinds sewed up, which virtually guaranteed success for everyone in our group.

The first Canadas came out of the reservation too high for anyone to shoot, and when Connie raised her gun to do so, I quietly but firmly urged her to hold off for a better opportunity. She didn't like it very well, but acquiesced to my request, commenting however, "We may not get another chance at a shot all day, and with all of those geese up there, I couldn't have missed." I then explained to her that several other much better chances would present themselves within the next two or three hours, at least up until ten o'clock or ten-thirty.

Twenty minutes later three more Canadas cruised out of the reserve, spotted our decoys, responded to our calling and began to circle. When they got within 30 yards of our pit and were only 20 yards off of the water, I gently told Connie to "take 'em." Fully expecting her to raise her gun and fire, I was aghast when she just sat there. Finally, when she still didn't react and the big birds began to move away, I got off a shot and dropped one at forty yards. Upon retrieving it, I carefully explained to Connie what she needed to do to bag a honker, namely to shoot when one gets within range of under 40 yards and lead it a lot if it is flying fast, a lot more than she would when shooting at a dove at the same distance. Being a good dove hunter, she appreciated the advice.

A half-hour later a single nine-pounder emerged and circled low over the blind, and I told my dear spouse to shoot. Still no results and no shot. This time I admonished her more sternly and stated that if she didn't shoot soon she very likely wouldn't get a honker that day. With this scolding, she commented, "I want to get in the blind with Jack as I think he won't be so cranky and I am certain he will help me bag a bigger goose than you are able to do and in a more pleasant manner." Jack Williams, being an instructor of biology and comparative anatomy at the local community college where I was employed at the time, and who had accompanied my son, Bob, and me on a number of pheasant hunts in Iowa as well as on waterfowl outings, is a soft-spoken gentleman of gentile disposition.

Of course, Jack, being in the next blind from ours, had witnessed each of the episodes which had denied Connie her goose. Within a half-hour after Connie had seated herself in the pit with Jack, an eight-pound Canada flew out of the reservation, and Jack began calling. The honker at first went on by too high, with Jack restraining my wife's eagerness to shoot. Then it began to slowly swing back toward the blind from the backside, and it was coming in low. When it got within 25 yards and Connie did not appear as though she was going to shoot, Jack bellowed at her at the top of his lungs, "SHOOT, WOMAN, SHOOT!" Connie cranked off a shot and missed, but when the goose swung around to the front of the blind and was four feet off of the water, 20 yards from the pit, she crumpled the bird clean and was one very proud woman when Jack's Golden Retriever brought it back in and laid it at her feet.

Don's wife, Connie, shows off a mount of a scaup (blue bill) shot in the mid-1960s at Turkey Creek Farm.

When I sauntered over to congratulate Connie for a fine performance and Jack for a masterful job of projecting his voice finally inducing her to pull the trigger, everyone seemed to agree that it was a highly successful but hilarious hunt.

Over 32 years of waterfowl hunting, I killed between 400 and 500 geese and about the same number of ducks at Turkey Creek Farm and a few other places. The cardinal rule is to take only close shots within 40 yards or less, but at times, especially later in the season, necessity may require that on occasion, especially in regard to honkers, longer shots may have to be taken. That's where the big 10-gauge or the 12-gauge with three-and-a-half-inch shells comes in very handy since these two guns will reach out at least 10 to 15 yards farther with a bigger payload and harder punch than a conventional shotgun. For years I used a Big Ten on geese and turkeys but as a 73-year-old senior citizen today, I have opted for a Benelli which chambers a three-and-a-half-inch shell which is ideal for both honkers and turkeys. It is also much lighter than the Big Ten and is much easier to handle.

NOT ONE, BUT TWO!

Don Lamm, 1979

Shortly AFTER my father-in law, a well-known and loved Sedalia Missourian, J.A. "Pete" Vinson retired in 1979, after having worked 37 years as an electrician and a crane operator at the Missouri Pacific Railroad Shops in Sedalia, Missouri, I asked him if he would like to try his luck at goose hunting at Turkey Creek Farm, Inc., a waterfowl club of which I was part owner, located adjacent to the big federal Swan Lake Wildlife Reservation in Chariton County, Missouri.

J.A. had hunted raccoons almost all of his life and was an expert at it, having earned a number of honors from the Sedalia Coon hunters' Association, and he said, "Yes, Don, I'd like to try my hand at knocking down a honker, but I've never tried it before, although I have shot a good many ducks."

A week later found us walking in the dark to my favorite blind of the club, known as Number One blind, which was out in the middle of a cornfield with a two-acre lake about two to three feet deep surrounding it. All of the club members liked to hunt it the most, and since I owned 40 percent of the operation and there were ten blinds on the 132 acres, I had control of four blinds each day. Thus, I had Number One blind available to myself and my friends frequently. While each blind was allowed four hunters, I always restricted mine to two so as to avoid overcrowding and the possibility of an accident.

Pete and I settled into the blind just shortly before dawn, and when we could begin shooting some teal came whipping low just about five feet above the water at a rapid pace. My A5 Browning semi-automatic 12-gauge and J.A.'s double barrel each barked twice, but no ducks fell. They had taken us by surprise as ducks in the early morning often do. Five minutes later two wood ducks zoomed in right in front of us, and we both shot; this time Pete nailed one.

103

Don Lamm and his next door neighbor, Virgil Bryan, display their limits of two honkers each taken at Turkey Creek Farm in 1988.

Then about ten minutes later, a drake mallard moved into range on my side of the blind, and I lowered the boom on him and he dropped within ten feet of the pit.

Then, 15 minutes later some gadwalls skirted our decoys, and we each added one of those to our tally. After that the duck activity ceased, and I told Pete that the geese would soon be coming out of the reservation, and I explained to him that when a honker did approach the blind that he needed to hold off shooting until it got quite close, because a goose always looks large even far away. I stepped off 40 yards and put a stick up in the water to give him an idea of about where the bird should be before he shot.

We waited for about 15 minutes and several honkers came out in a group and were beginning to descend low enough for us to prepare to shoot, when those infernal pests, the railroad hunters, skybusted a flock of geese which were going over them at the same time. They had shot at them well over a hundred yards high, and when they did so it caused the geese approaching us and all the other honkers in the area to raise up 20 or 30 yards, which meant that no one got a shot.

I explained to Pete how for years our club members had had trouble with the railroad hunters parking their cars on a country road three-quarters of a mile from the reservation and then walking down the railroad track which was on the west side of our property, and then shooting at geese ridiculously high up with number four buckshot. The use of buckshot was illegal; in fact, the use of any lead shot was illegal at that time. The railroad clods, who had no regard for the law, used it because they knew that every so often, after shooting in concert at flocks of high geese which continuously came out of the reservation over them until ten o'clock in the morning, a honker would tumble out of a flock, and the mob over on the track would cheer and yell like a bunch of unruly wild west cowboys.

Those of us in private clubs who liked to call our geese in close over decoys deplored the railroad hunters' actions, and we talked to the railroad officials about the problem, but they did nothing, afraid I suppose that if they prevented those scoundrels from hunting, their railroad might be sabotaged. Appeals to federal and state conservation officials concerning their outrageous actions had no effect either.

The railroaders also stood along the fence of our club property, and sometimes when one of our club members or a guest knocked down a goose and it fell anywhere close to the railroad track, say within 50 yards or closer, one of their dogs would run out and steal the goose before one of our dogs could get it, and since the clods wouldn't give their stolen goose up, it infuriated us. On more than one occasion as a result of these antics, threats were made to shoot dogs if they weren't held in check.

Another thing about the railroad hunters was that they were very poor callers of geese, and they were much more inclined to scare them away rather than otherwise. This lent itself to additional tension because it made our calling task much more difficult because of their obnoxious overcalling and terrible honking. Also the railroaders would sometimes jeer at us from the railroad track for not shooting at high geese as they did and for letting them get in low and close before shooting them. Our killing of a lot more geese every morning than they were able to put into their game bags irritated them.

So, in essence, there was really an undeclared cold war between us and them. One year our club had a $3,000 water pump completely shot up and burned, which damaged it completely beyond repair, and we were never able to prove who did it in spite of an extensive investigation by the sheriff of Chariton County.

Getting back to our hunt, within 20 minutes of the time the railroaders had spoiled our first chance at the geese, two more came out

This Canada, bagged at Turkey Creek Farm, became part of a Sunday dinner for Lamm in mid-November, 1984.

of the reservation and swung in low over the blind and then flew right over our heads at 40 yards. We both shot, and the one Pete had taken went into a long glide and hit the ground on Cuddy's club over across the road from Turkey Creek. Since the two clubs had a reciprocal agreement that any honker shot which fell on the other' property could be retrieved by the person who hit it, there was no problem about going over to get it. While retrieving a goose on the other club, the person doing so could not shoot at another live honker which might come over him during the retrieve.

In later years, beginning in the early 1990s, Cuddy's was taken over by new owners, and they hardened their attitude about reciprocal retrieving and took the position that anything shot on our club which came over on them was theirs and vice versa. Indeed, honker hunting is one of the most territorial activities of mankind, and men jealously guard their space almost to the point of fanaticism.

Anyway, I walked over to Cuddy's, shot and retrieved Pete's goose about 75 yards in the soybean field, and upon returning to the blind we weighed the prize which tipped the scales at eight pounds. Another 20 minutes then went by, and a single goose emerged from the reservation yelping loudly. As sometimes occurred, it went over two or three of the other blinds and was shot at and missed. I called with all of the know-how I possessed, and the honker swung around in a big loop and headed straight in toward my side of the blind. At 35 yards, I cranked off a shot and the bird crumpled almost falling into the pit. Of course, I was pleased with the nine-pounder and the way I was able to bag it.

I then decided to do something that I had never done before in the 11 years which I had been a member of the club. I told Pete that I was going to walk over and associate with the railroad hunters which would give him time to bag another goose by himself while I was away from the blind.

My intentions were to pose as another railroader in order to gain a measure of their ideas and thinking, so I walked over a half-mile directly south of our club and then cut over west to the railroad track and then north down the track to the hunters. As I approached, we exchanged pleasantries, and I asked them how they were doing and they said that they had gotten one which was "way up there when we popped it."

I made no comment to this statement, and as I observed them I noticed that they were calling far too often and too much, and when geese did come over they skybusted at them way too high. I shot once or twice, too, to make them think that I was one of them. At that time, I said nothing to signify how I felt about their goose hunting conduct.

Finally, after staying there for an hour, I decided that it was time to go, and I got up and climbed over the fence to go into Turkey Creek. I'll never forget the look on their faces when I did that. They emphatically said, "Hey, you can't go in there. It's a private club owned by a bunch of rich, arrogant and snotty doctors and they'll see that the club caretaker will kick you out on your rear end or they'll have you arrested." I then told them firmly that I owned 40 percent of the club, that were no doctors in it, and while a few of the members were wealthy, I was not one of them, being just an instructor of economics and psychology at a community college in Sedalia.

I also then explained to them that they were breaking the law by shooting buckshot at geese, they were shooting at honkers much too high which was frustrating and annoying everyone, that their dogs were grabbing geese which were not theirs, and that their calling was atrocious, scaring away more geese than coaxing them in. I explained to them if they would correct these things, everyone, in-

107

cluding themselves, would get more birds.

As I left, I backed away from them with my head facing them with my gun ready, as I feared that one of them might decide to shoot me and I didn't relish taking on a load of lead in my back. Of course, what I said to them had no results whatsoever, because for the next 10 or 12 years the railroaders continued to practice their stupid polemics and plague us. In the early 1990s when the goose hunting deteriorated drastically in the Swan Lake area, the railroad hunters no longer showed up to hunt adjacent to the reservation or along the western border of our club, and the problem solved itself.

While walking back across Turkey Creek toward our blind, when I was about 200 yards from it, I noticed a large Canada which had emerged from the reservation and was headed for Pete in the blind. I immediately got flat on the ground so that the goose wouldn't see me and flair off, and since there were no honkers headed over the skybusters, things looked good for Pete. The honker swung around in front of him but was too far away. Then it veered over to the side of the pit and suddenly changed course and flew straight over the blind at about 35 yards. J.A.'s 12 barked and the goose folded, splashing the water approximately 15 yards from him. We certainly didn't have to go across the road to Cuddy's for that magnificent 10-pounder, which was later mounted by Anthony Eddy, renowned taxidermist of Slater, Missouri, and it graced Pete's bedroom wall until his death on November 29, 1982, while he was out in the woods coon hunting.

So, on that late fall day in 1979, on his first goose hunt, J.A. got not just one goose, but two! Also, on the hunt, together we nailed five ducks as a bonus, because when I got to the blind after he shot that big second goose, he also had added another drake mallard to the game bag while I was conversing with the railroad hunter spoilers. Also, the spoilers had not prevented me from getting a honker except that the time I spent with them would have been better spent in the blind where I might have gotten a second honker that morning as Pete did.

MEL'S LAST HUNT,
SWAN SONG OF A GREAT CAREER AFIELD

Richard Cooper, 1981

I HAD THE PRIVILEGE and sweet sorrow of taking my great father-in-law, Mel Shearburn, on his last hunt. It was early November of 1981, and Mel had turned 77 the preceding July. He was so badly hobbled by circulatory problems in his legs that he could scarcely walk a block without having to stop and rest. His days in the field pursuing quail had ended a few years before, even though the fire and enthusiasm for the sport was still there.

I asked him if he would be willing to try goose hunting as a substitute where very little walking would be required. He snapped up the offer quickly, and I immediately began making preparations for a trip to the Swan Lake National Wildlife Refuge in Chariton County, Missouri.

My good friend, Don Lamm, was part owner of a goose hunting club just south of the refuge boundary. The club had ten blinds, all numbered, and he owned four of them. The blind which each owner was allowed to shoot from rotated each day of the week throughout the season.

Guests of owners were allowed to hunt, and Don had told me that I was welcome to use one of his blinds any time. Just let him know what date. I had taken advantage of this offer several times before.

Since it was usually crowded on weekends, I decided that it might be best if Mel and I went on a weekday. As it turned out, the rotation had Don assigned to the best blind of the club on a Wednesday. I confirmed everything with him, and the day before Mel and his wife drove from their home in Bronaugh to where my wife and I lived in Sedalia.

Early the next morning, Mel and I headed out on the nearly 70-mile trip to Turkey Creek Farm, which was the name of Don's club.

Mel's somber expression belies his wonderful personality and personal satisfaction after his last hunt, a goose hunting caper at Turkey Creek Farm, November 4, 1981.

The only obstacle to the hunt was getting from the club's parking lot to our blind, but Mel had a solution for that. He carried a heavy plastic trash bag with him, and when he needed to take a rest, he would spread the bag before him and kneel on it until he was ready to proceed farther. The bag was necessary because the ground was extremely muddy. After four rest stops, we reached the blind, and there was only the slightest suggestion of dawn beginning to show in the eastern sky.

We loaded up and would be ready when the morning flight started. Mel agreed to use my Browning Light Twelve, feeling that his trusty 20-gauge A5 might be a little light for such armor-plated game as a Canada goose. I was using a 16-gauge Fox Model BST side-by-side double, a bit light for geese possibly, but that morning it proved to be quite adequate.

The sky was heavily clouded, and the threat of rain was in the air. Fortunately, it held off until we had finished the hunt.

It was almost fully daylight when the flights of yelping geese started pouring out of the refuge headed for nearby fields of waste grain. They were much too high for any shooting, so for nearly an hour we watched the undersides of close to a thousand geese.

Finally, a discombobulated goose spied the decoys in front of our blind and decided to settle in amongst what he perceived to be some of his contented friends. We did not use calls since, being rank amateurs, we knew that we would only scare geese off rather than attract them.

I whispered to Mel to wait until the goose was committed to landing before he shot. When the landing gear came down and the wings reached for a last bite of air, Mel took him, and he had his daily limit in one shot.

I waded out in the shallow water in my hip boots and retrieved a medium-sized Canada.

About 30 minutes later, we had a repeat performance, and it was my turn to score, although my goose was noticeably smaller than his.

As we drove back to Sedalia, we talked over the morning's hunt, marveling at the thousands of geese we had seen. It was a great day.

Also, it was one which cost me a day's pay since I had taken off from my classes at Smith-Cotton High School. When I told the principal what I was going to do, he said that he couldn't authorize a day of personal leave for that type of absence even though he would like to. Still, he understood because he was a hunter, too.

It was a privilege to be with Mel Shearburn on his last hunt, a hunt that we managed to squeeze in despite his failing health. He was truly one of the great men in my life.

Mel died in July 1985, just a few days short of his 81st birthday.

NOTHING LIKE A PEELED BACK GUN BARREL TO SCARE ONE TO DEATH

Don Lamm, late 1970s

IT WAS a warm November Saturday morning in the late 1970s which found several of my colleagues and myself in the goose blinds at Turkey Creek Farm, Inc., a waterfowl club of which I was part owner, located adjacent to the big Swan Lake Wildlife Reservation in Chariton County, Missouri.

Among my friends there that day was Walter E. Diehl, a professor of psychology at Central Methodist College, Fayette, Missouri, and a person with whom I worked under while he was a vice-principal and I was a teacher in the social science department at Smith-Cotton High School, Sedalia, Missouri. I also had gone on pheasant hunts with him in the early 1960s in Kansas and Nebraska. He was an enthusiastic upland bird and waterfowl hunter.

He was down in one of the levy blinds of the club next to the reservation, and I was in one of the back blinds about a quarter of a mile from him. About nine-thirty, three honkers cruised out of the reservation yelping at about 45 yards high right over Walt's pit, and he cut down on them with his J.C. Higgins pump 12-gauge which he had purchased many years before at Sears Roebuck for $49.95 and which he says was a highly reliable firearm which patterned well, was light and easy to handle.

After he shot, a large honker fell out of the sky and sailed down into the water-soaked field about 70 yards from his blind. Since he had no retrieving dog and no one else on the scene had one either, Walt climbed out of the pit to retrieve the bird himself. Of course, as he got closer to the bird, the more rapidly it walked away from him in order to get away.

The closer Walt finally got to the goose, the faster he was sliding around in the water-soaked mud, and eventually he fell down hard and his gun went down with him. He immediately righted himself and continued his pursuit of the Canada until he got within 30 yards of it, and then he steadied himself to shoot, fully expecting the bird to topple over dead.

However, instead, the gun made a peculiar muffled cracking sound, and Walt fell down again. Upon getting up, I noticed that his gun barrel was completely peeled back a full six inches with metal slivers protruding from it all around in a circle. I then jumped out of my blind, checked to see whether he had been hurt. Discovering he hadn't, I then shot his downed goose and walked back to his blind with him.

I explained to him that I had an extra gun he could use to bag a second goose, but he said in a shaky voice, "Don, will you please shoot that extra honker for me? I'm so unglued right now, I couldn't hit an elephant if it sat right on top of me." I was soon able to shoot another honker, and then we went to lunch and ate some chilli.

Some weeks later I hunted with Walt again at Turkey Creek Farm and he had a brand new J.C. Higgins 12-gauge, similar but updated to the one which had blown up due to mud having lodged itself in the barrel when he had fallen the first time. Walt had a six-inch poly choke put on his older Higgins which had exploded, and today he uses it as a backup gun.

Since that day over 20 years ago, I have fallen down several times in the mud while hunting birds of all kinds, and I have always remembered what happened to Walt that day at the goose club. As a result, I always check the end of my gun barrel immediately after getting up from a fall, and on two or three occasions I have found it partially or fully plugged up with dirt or mud. Thus, I always carry a knife to get it out, and I also sometimes take the gun apart and blow down the barrel. Of course, Walt now does likewise!

The fear and embarrassment hunting colleague Walt Diehl must have experienced after blowing up his old J.C. Higgins 12-gauge pursuing a crippled Canada goose on Turkey Creek Farm in the late 1970s.

A WARM END TO A COLD GOOSE HUNT

Richard Cooper, 1978

MY YOUNGER SON, Eric, got his introduction to goose hunting on a cold and damp late November day in 1978. Since he was just nine years old at the time and about a couple of years away from carrying a shotgun on his own, he went along as an observer. We were guests of Don Lamm at his goose hunting club, Turkey Creek Farm, in Chariton County, Missouri near the Swan Lake National Wildlife Refuge.

We drove in separate vehicles so that if we wanted to leave for home earlier than Don, or vice versa, the other wouldn't be inconvenienced.

We were located in one of the better blinds of the club, and Don situated himself in another. We stayed put in our blind, but Don moved around to other blinds when slack times developed in the number of geese flying. Since it was late in the season and a heavily clouded day with the threat of cold rain or snow, there were very few club members or guests around. Consequently, most blinds were available to anyone who wanted to use them.

Lots of geese were flying, but they stayed at a safe altitude well out of range despite the fact that weather conditions were the kind that you associate with low-flying birds. The experience of being targets for most of the season had educated them about maintaining a good margin of safety above the surrounding countryside as they came yelping out of the refuge heading for nearby grain fields in the morning feeding ritual.

Nearly all were Canadas, with a very small sprinkling of Giant Canadas. This strain of goose, once thought to be nearly extinct, has made a remarkable comeback in the Mississippi flyway.

Around 9:30, a Giant Canada came in from the south flying low on its way back into the refuge. Eric spotted him first and nearly exploded with a throaty whisper, "Dad, look!" It was quite a sight, a huge bird that got bigger with each wingbeat as it fought its way against an increasing north wind. It was somewhat like suddenly seeing a B-52 covered with feathers and bearing a white cheek patch. At about 35 yards, I cut down with my 16-gauge double loaded with magnum 2s. There was a clear and distinct "splat" as the pellets bounced off the Giant Canada's armor plate of feathers without a sign of any damage done. I was nonplussed by its complete disregard for my accurate shooting. I re-aimed and cranked off a second shot while it was still well within range. Again, a distinct "splat" confirmed that I was on target, but the undisturbed giant never missed a wingbeat as it cruised on to its destination inside the refuge.

I looked at Eric, and he looked at me. I don't recall what I said after the disheartening experience, but I am sure that "tough bird" would be an insufficient description.

I was using a 16-gauge because federal steel shot regulations were just being implemented, and they did not yet apply to 16-gauge guns. It gave me an opportunity to use up the last of a box of number 2 lead shot which I had purchased at a bargain counter a couple years before. Looking back, it was probably not a very wise thing to do, considering how toxic lead pellets have proven to be to feeding waterfowl. However, in an effort to save a few bucks, that is why I was using a 16-gauge.

After the deflating experience with the Giant Canada, the number of geese flying decreased considerably. Combining that development with an increasing north wind and a further drop in the temperature made life in our blind less and less enjoyable.

Don dropped by after a few more minutes carrying a good-sized Canada he had gotten on the other side of the club. He said that he was heading home, leaving us with only one other party on the property.

Eric and I agreed to stay no more than two additional hours; if we had nothing by that time, we, too, would head for home.

Finally, at about 11:30, a discombobulated Canada broke off from its flight going out to feed and headed back to the refuge, crossing low right in front of our blind. Again, the 16-gauge spoke, and this time it had the authority to drop the goose onto a grassy bank about 60 yards from the blind. It had been a long, cold morning of frustration, but success was finally ours. The three Ps of hunting success had worked again.

117

Eric and I headed back to the parking lot with the north wind nagging at our camouflage parkas. Oh, to get my truck started and some heat into the cab as quickly as possible!

Before we left the parking lot, however, I unlimbered my tripod and camera and insisted on a few pictures. This has always been a passion of mine even though it is an inconvenience and sometimes, to some, an irritating delay. I have always maintained that in the future all parties involved will be glad that the time and effort were taken to record the event on film. As the years have passed, no one that I have photographed on our many hunting trips has ever regretted that it was done.

Richard with son, Eric, and a large Canada goose bagged at Turkey Creek Farm on a wet and cold day, November 12, 1978.

There was only one other vehicle in the parking lot, a pickup with camper at the far end. As I was storing the camera and tripod, a figure emerged from the camper and motioned for us to come over. I got Eric from the cab which was still hardly warm, and we walked toward the figure which continued to stand outside the camper. As we made the nearly 75-yard walk, a few flakes of snow began to sting our faces.

By the time we were halfway to the camper, the husky figure began to look familiar. When we arrived, my hunch was confirmed. It was Walt Diehl, a former teaching colleague in Sedalia in the 1960s, and at that time a counselor and psychologist at Missouri Military Academy in Mexico, Missouri. I hadn't seen him for at least 20 years. Don had failed to tell me that he was going to try for a goose that morning.

The pickup/camper belonged to Cecil Hamilton, Walt's next door neighbor, and the two were just preparing to sit down to a midday meal of Hamburger Helper. They invited us in, and we shared a platter of the delicacy with them. Considering how windy and cold it was outside, nothing could have been more satisfying and comforting than a plate of steaming Hamburger Helper inside Cecil's toasty warm camper.

We must have spent nearly 45 minutes breaking bread with them and swapping stories about our successes and disappointments of the morning. Then Eric and I thanked them for their much appreciated hospitality and hot-footed it back through the wind-driven snow to our pickup.

Eventually we got the cab warm, but I think that surely some of the heat must have come back with us inside our clothing, thanks to Cecil's wonderfully comfortable propane heated camper.

MIRED IN THE MUD PURSING A GOOSE

Don Lamm, 1981

YEARS AGO in the early 1980s my wife, Connie, and I went up to Turkey Creek Farm, Inc., our goose and duck hunting club adjacent to the Swan Lake Federal Reservation in Chariton County, Missouri.

It was a damp, chilly, windy late fall afternoon, and there obviously had been a lot of rain in the area in recent days. On this particular day the geese were flying over the property across the road from our club in considerable numbers, so we asked the club members over there at Cuddy's if we could hunt the back of their place farthest from the reservation. They gave us permission, and we soon were under cover in a fence row.

About 45 minutes went by and then three geese came over low enough to attempt a knock-down. We both shot and a honker fell out, but rather than descend straight down close to us, it sailed out into the muddy field, hit the ground about 65 yards out, and then began to walk away. Connie said, "Oh, my stars, we really do need a retrieving dog, Don." I replied, "We can manage without one — I'll be the dog." My intention was to walk out there slowly upon the goose and shoot it on the ground when I got within 30 yards of it, as I had done on a number of instances before.

Well, after getting 40 yards out into the field with much difficulty because of the sticky-mucky mud, and the goose now still too far away to shoot at since it was continuing to move away, I became completely mired down and couldn't move nor could I get my waders off. I yelled to Connie for some help, and she, being much lighter than I, came out slowly to me and helped me squeeze out of my waist-high rubber boots with much groaning and grunting. She then picked them up and began to carry them back to the fence row where we had set up at the beginning of our little hunt. I followed her back completely barefooted with the coldest bare feet that one can imagine.

120

One might ask, Don, since you and Connie owned 40 percent of Turkey Creek Farm, Inc., for over 30 years and hunted it many times four days a week, why in heaven's name didn't you have at least one or two well-trained retrieving dogs? The answer is simple. In addition to my waterfowl hunting during all of these years, I was also an avid dove, quail and pheasant hunter, and Connie and I had two English setters, our favorite breed of hunting dog. Considering the fact that other club members at Turkey Creek had good retrieving dogs, plus the fact that my assessments to maintain the club and to pump water into the lakes amounted to four times that of the other members, we felt that the additional expense of one or two retrieving dogs was unjustified with our relatively limited amount of income. But, on the day I froze my feet in the slimy, slippery mud, a good retrieving dog would have been a godsend and would have more than earned its room and board. Of course, since Connie and I were hunting well over a half-mile from Turkey Creek Farm late in the afternoon, no dog from one of our own club members was available. Also, we didn't anticipate the sticky mud fiasco in the first place, but on later occasions we sized up the mud factor much more carefully under Connie's watchful eye.

By the way, the honker got away and probably became a delicious dinner for a coyote or fox.

THE GALLOPING TOM
THAT ALMOST GOT AWAY

Don Lamm, 1978

IN THE LATE 1970s after I had only killed a few turkeys, my son, Bob, age 22 at the time, took me on an outing early one April morning south of Cole Camp, Missouri, which has remained etched in my memory ever since.

Being a superb caller, after first using his own hands as an owl hoot, he was able to elicit a gobble about a quarter of a mile away. We crept up to within 125 yards of the gobbler's roost, and both of us then positioned ourselves behind two large trees in our well-camouflaged outfits and waited. Soon, Bob gave some soft yelps, and we silently waited some more. After several more calls some of the birds finally flew down off the roost.

The next task was to separate a gobbler from the hens, but after many subtle attempts nothing worked, and the turks wandered off into the woods. After they got about a quarter of a mile away, Bob felt that we still had a good chance of isolating a gobbler, so we continued to follow them, calling every so often and getting an occasional gobble in return. That was enough to convince Bob, who because of his experience was calling the moves on the hunt, that we had a chance to get a gobbler.

The birds continued to amble away from us in spite of all varieties of calling, but after another several hundred yards of pursuit, Bob motioned for me to hang back and he would move up a block or so and make some calls. I waited and waited, keeping ever alert, and then Bob came forth with one of the weirdest turkey cackles I had ever heard! Then absolute silence for five full minutes. I was beginning to think we had again been abandoned.

However, such was not the case. I flinched at the roar of Bob's big Ithaca 10-gauge, borrowed from me, which was then followed by another thunderous shot. Then I heard some leaves rustling combined with Bob's shout of, "Get him Dad, get him, he's coming your way!" Looking up, I saw the big gobbler running rapidly, actually galloping would best describe it, about 50 yards away. I cut down on him with my A5 Browning semi-automatic 12-gauge, but my two and three-quarter-inch shells made no contact, and the bird disappeared down into a wooded valley.

Of course, Bob was very depressed at having made two inadequate shots at 35 yards with the Big Ten, neither of which killed the bird. He then said that even though the bird was wounded, he felt that there was absolutely no chance of finding it, considering the speed at which the bird had galloped away.

I looked at him and said, "I disagree. Considering the fact that the turk ran straight down into that wooded valley, I think we should take a half an hour for a good look. He could well be down there at the bottom incapacitated." Bob reluctantly assented and we began searching.

Within 15 minutes and a quarter of a mile down into the valley, I looked ahead 25 yards and spotted the gobbler lying right out in the open on the ground between Bob and myself. I told Bob, "There he is, lying there between us!"

"Where? Where?," he exclaimed.

"Right there in front of you less than 20 yards away — get ready to shoot."

"I still don't see it, Dad."

Just at that moment the bird jumped up rapidly and began running. This time my A5 did its job and finished him off. Of course, Bob was elated as was I.

I then told him that since he didn't kill the bird with his two good chances with the Big Ten, and since he had a chance to shoot the bird a third time but couldn't see it right in front of his face, I was going to put the 22-pound bird in my game bag and take it home. He gave me no argument. Of course, at that time I had only killed five turkeys in five years and he had shot at least 30. As of this writing, July 23, 2000, I have killed 30 and he has shot well over a hundred, since he hunts gobblers each year in Missouri and Kansas and sometimes in Tennessee.

There are two lessons to be derived from this story. One is that while turkeys are often very hard to kill, a wounded turk, especially if it is shot within 40 yards, is well worth diligently looking for a

"The galloping tom that almost got away." Both Don's son, Bob, left, and he laid claim to the prize since each had a hand in shooting it.

long time before giving up. Also, as every gobbler hunter knows, a head shot is by far the best part of the turkey's anatomy to opt for rather than the big bird's body. Of course, one's gun should be patterned occasionally to make certain that it is still accurate. The other lesson to be gleaned from this narrative is that it pays to follow up on turkeys when they come off of the roost and won't come in close enough for a shot. If one stays far enough back and persists in his pursuit without being seen, sooner or later a gobbler will respond and present himself, even though it may be several hours into the day.

HUNG UP ON NUMBER 13, THE "PEEK-A-BOO" BIRD

Don Lamm, 1988

BY 1986, I HAD BEEN hunting turkeys for 12 or 13 years and during that time, I had bagged 12 gobblers, my best weighing in at 26-3/4 pounds with an 11-inch beard, with my brother-in-law, Virgil Tagtmeyer, having assisted me in calling him down from the roost one April morning about six forty-five a.m. The killing of this particular bird proved to be classic all the way in regard to the use of the owl hoot call, the gobble of the bird from the roost, the turk flying down from the roost, the set-up regarding my shooting position as suggested by Virgil and the 40-yard shot with my Ithaca 10-gauge itself which dropped the huge gobbler dead in his tracks.

Prior to his coming down from the roost, some adroit calling by Tagtmeyer indeed proved instrumental in the gobbler's approaching close enough for a good shot. After shooting the bird, we guessed him at 23 pounds, but at the check in station, surprisingly it proved to be considerably more, as mentioned above. It had markedly long spurs, and the tips of its wings also revealed signs of many a sparring match with other male birds. Most of the gobblers I had shot in my spring hunts only during these 12 or 13 years had taken place within 30 or 40 miles south of Sedalia, Missouri in the company of my son, Bob, and Virgil. Both Bob and Virgil probably rank as two of the best gobbler hunters in the state, having had years of experience.

When I first began hunting turks, for the first five years I was exceptionally lucky. I killed one each year for those first five years the first time out and I began to think, "This is easy as pie." Some of my colleagues were experiencing tough luck by having their birds hang up and not coming in range, wandering off with their hens, or outright missing their shots, even at close range. Concerning the latter, when I heard about it, I thought to myself, "How could anyone miss a target that big within 30 to 40 yards?"

Well, within the next three years I was to find out. To make a long story short, I got no gobblers either on the first or second week of the spring season. At that time, I had not begun to hunt in the fall because I didn't think I had a remote chance of getting one. On those spring turks, I began to miss some good shots either because I moved a little just at the critical time or because I didn't have my gun fully ready when the gobbler exposed himself out in the open. They would duck their heads and run off faster than one could say SCAT, and whatever shot I got off was six feet behind them!

Then things picked up, and over the next few years I was able to score on seven more birds, all nice ones 19 pounds or better with no jakes. After shooting bird number 12, a 21-1/2-pounder on a thrilling hunt in deep woods with Virgil, who also got a big gobbler that morning, my confidence in myself was reinforced. I had the feet, tail and wings of the bird blended into a wall mount which is now downstairs in my bird trophy room, along with many others I have shot over these many years.

The next spring, I went out with no luck during both weeks of the spring season in which one bird was allowed each week. The same thing occurred the next spring, and I suddenly realized, "My God, I'm hung up on number 13!" I had never believed that 13 could be an unlucky number for anyone under any circumstances, but I had now become a believer, and a rather bitter one, to tell the truth.

At the beginning of the next spring season, the third year of my "dry gobbler spell," I discussed all of this with my good friend and neighbor across the road from me, Virgil Bryan, who had let me hunt previously on his 180-acre farm near Florence, Missouri. He said he had recently heard turks calling in the woods and had also seen some in the bottom.

Early the next day found the two of us at the farm. We split, with Virgil going down into the bottom and my heading into the woods, the two hunting sites being on opposite sides of the farm. I walked cautiously in the dark up the road leading through the woods, taking great care not to spook any birds. This was successful, and I reached the area where I had seen and had hunted them in previous years. I then gave an owl hoot. No response. Another hoot. This time a gobble at about 165 yards. I stealthily moved up 35 yards and found a large oak tree to sit down and lean up against, although I would have preferred the center of a well-filled-out cedar tree.

I then emitted a couple of soft yelps from my "Easy Yelper" call, remained silent and listened. No gobble, but I could hear some hens clucking. Fifteen minutes later, another call from me but no response. Then after ten more minutes, a gobbler flew down from the roost as did three hens, and I gave some yelps on my call again, hoping that the first gobbler or some other gobbler would pick up on them and begin gobbling and coming in. However, instead of that occurring, several other birds flew down from the roost, but none came my way; in fact, they began moving away from me up through the woods.

I knew then, due to the fact that I am no expert caller, that any chance of coaxing in a gobbler out of that group of birds was nil and I would have to find another way. The birds were well over a hundred yards away from me, and not having spotted me, they leisurely headed into a part of the woods with which I was familiar. Rather than make a loop in an attempt to come up on them from the opposite side, I decided to keep them in sight and hope that they might stop at a place to feed, dust or rest, at which time I might be able to get one of the three gobblers to respond to my call and come toward me.

I concealed myself in a cedar tree, which allowed me to remain standing so that I could better observe the birds which at that moment were out of sight, and I gave a soft call. An immediate gobble! Another yelp and another response, and this time I saw the bird's head peeking slightly above some heavy buck brush at about 60 yards. I raised my big Ithaca 10-gauge and readied it for a shot at closer range the next time I called.

I waited several minutes and then gave a purr on my "Easy Yelper," and this time the gobbler came out of the brush with its head visible and gobbled, but it was still too far away to risk a shot, and it also darted back into that infernal brush too rapidly. The next time in this peek-a-boo fiasco, the bird emerged only for a split second from the brush at 50 yards. While I had the Big Ten up and ready, the range was still too great for a guaranteed kill, and the bird was not actually sufficiently clear of the brush to enable me to get a clear-cut shot.

By this time my arm was aching from holding up the 11-pound gun for so long in an attempt to get off a good shot at just the right moment. I said to my self, "Is this monstrous peek-a-boo bird ever going to fully cooperate? Will it eventually run away and I'll never see it again? Or will I break the number 13 jinx and take it triumphantly back to the car, or will I return empty handed?"

The illusive 21-3/4-pound "peek-a-boo" gobbler taken by Lamm in 1988 just east of Florence, Missouri. Note the 11-pound Ithaca 10-gauge used to bring him down.

Returning empty-handed was unthinkable!

One more time the gobbler went through its antics in the manner described above, only this time it was a bit closer to me at 45 yards, but it ducked back into its buck brush haven before I could sufficiently level off on its head. Finally, following one more cluck on the call, Mr, Peek-a-Boo stepped a full five yards out into the open, completely clear of the brush. I cut down on him and saw him leap into the brush and I said to myself; "This obnoxious, exhausting gobbler has peek-a-booed me again, this time for good." However, when I reached the place where I had seen him plunge into the brush, there he was, into it, stone dead.

I was overjoyed that I had finally broken the number 13 jinx and that I had outwitted a foxy turkey, the 21-3/4-pound peek-a-boo bird. Virgil, too, shared his elation with me saying, "Don, it took you a good while to bag that bird. I've been back here at the truck for an hour with the gobbler I got down in the bottom early this morning, but it wasn't a hide-and-seeker."

As I have grown older over the years, I have graduated to lighter guns than the big 10-gauges. Some years ago, I sold my two 10-gauges to my son Bob, who uses them on both turks and geese, but I find that my 12-gauge Benelli, with its three-and-a-half-inch shells and other special features, is much more suited to my purpose. Had I had the Benelli at the time I shot the peek-a-boo bird, the task would have been much easier.

THE APPLE ORCHARD TOM ...
MY FAVORITE MOUNT

Don Lamm, circa 1990

SOME YEARS AGO, my older son, Art, and I decided to open up the second week of the spring turkey season together at a farm located about 12 miles south of Syracuse, Missouri, which he had hunted in the past with good results. During the first week, Art had gotten a 21-pound gobbler, but I had not yet scored so I was eager to shoot one.

Before daylight found us in a woods which supported mostly large oak trees and some big cedars, some quite dense. Art stationed himself about 115 yards over to my left at the foot of a giant white oak where he had shot gobblers two years previously, while I crouched behind a well-filled-out cedar. As Art soon began calling, he told me later he had spied a couple of Toms with four hens about a hundred yards distant, but try as he might, he couldn't coax any of the male birds in close enough for a shot.

As time went by, I surmised that Art was having difficulty, and I began calling on my "Easy Yelper" call. After ten minutes, I heard a gobble some 200 yards away over to my right. After several minutes of silence, I hit the call again but with no response. Fifteen minutes later, I heard rustling in the leaves about 20 yards from me which came from the center of the dense cedar grove. I looked and looked, but so help me, Hannah, I couldn't see what it was, but I strongly suspected that it almost had to be a turk, hopefully a big gobbler!

After several minutes elapsed while I carefully listened and peered into the grove, I gave a soft purr on my call and, lo and behold, the bird gobbled loudly, and from that I could tell that it was on the opposite side of a large, thick cedar only 20 yards directly in front of me. I strained my eyes to get a glimpse of it, but to no avail, so I soon clucked with the call, hoping the turk would step out into the open. No luck there, but it did gobble again louder than ever. I was so tense that I think my heart was thumping louder than Mr. Tom was gobbling!

This scenario continued for a number of minutes, my calling very softly, the Tom now gobbling loudly at nearly every call, but with no appearance of the "Invisible Creature." Even intervals of absolute silence didn't work. It was obvious that I should have put out a decoy at the time I originally set up. Anyway, since I had been crouched there for so long, I was tempted to step rapidly out of my cover and rush the turk's tree, but I knew if I did so, he would either hear me or see me and would flush, keeping the big cedar between me and him as a grouse often does, and I wouldn't have a Chinaman's chance to get a bead on him under any circumstances. So the only solution, in my mind, was to try harder to coax him out from behind that tree, as I had done a few years earlier in a similar situation as clearly enumerated in the story in this book entitled, "Hung Up On Number 13, The Peek-a-Boo Bird."

My calling and the turk's gobbling continued for another few minutes, and then all of a sudden a large coyote appeared only 10 yards from me charging that turk's tree rapidly. I was tempted to shoot that predator, but I wanted the turkey a lot more, and I figured that perhaps if the coyote caught the gobbler I could kill them both with my big Ithaca 10-gauge and walk out with two trophies! But such was not to be; the Tom flushed in haste and I never even saw it, and the coyote disappeared in the thick cedars. Incidentally, on several occasions while gobbler hunting, I have observed coyotes closely nearby, which proves, I believe, that they prey on a good many turks each year, especially hens and jakes. My guess is it's a real contest between a mature gobbler and a mature coyote, since both are so incredibly intelligent and endowed with such keen senses.

Following that incident, Art and I went over to another place about four miles away. It was now 9:30 a.m. ,and soon we were on a ridge. Art started glassing another ridge over a quarter of a mile away, which had some open areas in the woods containing patches of low weeds, lespedeza, and some sprinklings of semi-dense switch grass. Art then handed me his binoculars and commented, "Hey, Dad, look over to the left of that large hickory tree about 15 yards in that open space, I'm certain there's a big gobbler there." He was correct; there he was with a couple of hens.

Art then suggested that we make a big loop and quietly come up on them from the top of the ridge, making certain we were not seen. Twenty minutes later saw us within 125 yards of where we had spotted the turks. We each found a large tree to sit down in front of facing in the direction of the birds, and after listening carefully for a few minutes, Art then began to call.

At first there was no reaction, but after two or three more soft yelps with intervals of silence in between, a gobbler answered and he began to move in rather rapidly. From where I was, I couldn't see him, but Art could. When the bird got within 40 yards, Art whispered to me, "Take him, Dad." But so help me, the switch grass and other cover still prevented me from spotting the bird. I whispered back to Art, "I can't see him; you get him." His 12-gauge Winchester pump, which he had used with great effectiveness on many kinds of game birds, roared, and I then finally saw the Tom kicking in the grass 35 yards away. We were both happy that our "binocular" stalk had been such a success, except that Art was sorry that he had gotten the shot at the gobbler instead of me. Over the years, he has killed at least three times as many turkeys as I have, and he's always happy when I nail one.

It was now approaching 11:00 a.m., and I needed to bag myself a gobbler. Art said that he knew another place where he thought I might have a chance to get one ... on Farmer Jones' land five miles away. We drove up to an empty house and, upon getting out, there was an apple orchard about 80 yards distant with about half knee-high grass cover in it. We split up temporarily as we approached the orchard very cautiously from two sides. Suddenly, I saw a big gobbler step out in the open at the edge of an apple tree 60 yards in front of me, and if I had been close enough I could have killed it right there.

When this happened, Art was away from me about 70 yards, intending to rendezvous with me in the far corner of the large orchard. So I couldn't communicate with him without spooking the bird, which had run back into the grass out of sight. I thought it had seen me, but such apparently was not the case. I carefully moved up another 20 yards into a weedy fence row bordering the orchard, knelt down and gave a soft cluck on my call. No reaction. I was quite certain he was still there ... another cluck or purr might induce him to come out again. Sure enough, it did, and at 40 yards I lowered the boom on him with my Big Ten Ithaca and the bird toppled over. Art then yelled at me, "What did you shoot at?" and I remarked,

"Art, I nailed what I am sure is a really nice gobbler right out at the orchard's edge at 40 yards." He and I then went to it, and it was absolutely a magnificent specimen. Its black feathers composed of different hues, shone brilliantly in the bright sunlight, its beard was full and long, and its large red, white and blue head was impressive.

Don's three-year-old daughter, Carrie, seems thrilled to share the spotlight with two big gobblers bagged by her father and brother in 1981. Don's bird, background, weighed 19 pounds. Art's bird tipped the scales at 22-1/2 pounds.

When we took our gobblers to the check-in station in Morgan County, Art's bird weighed in at 22 pounds and mine at 23-1/4. He is the second largest gobbler I have gotten in my 20-some odd years of turkey hunting. My largest of the 28 I have killed as of February 6, 2000, tipped the scales at 26-3/4 pounds. Nine months later I picked up the full strut mount of the 23-pounder from Anthony Eddy, a taxidermist who lives in Slater, Missouri, and who has received many awards over the years for his immaculate and superior work. It is one of the finest trophies I possess among the many which I have accumulated over the past 50 years.

I am indeed fortunate to have two fine sons, Art and Bob, with whom I hunt a number of times each year in my now golden years. Both of them are very savvy at turkey, waterfowl and upland bird hunting, and I owe both of them a big debt for contributing to many of my most cherished hunting memories. The camaraderie which we now have and have had far back into the past is beyond compare and is something that money simply can never buy.

"IT WAS 60 YARDS AWAY, YOU FOOL"

Don Lamm, Early 1990s

IT WAS A BEAUTIFUL April morning in the early 1990s that found my son, Bob, and I about 13 miles southeast of Sedalia, Missouri, listening to a big Tom turkey gobble while perched on a limb in a large sycamore tree close to a creek. Bob had scouted the bird the night before and had told me that I had a good chance of adding number 19 to my gobbler scoreboard if I could keep my cool and do what he said.

I was more than eager, since I didn't take any time to scout due to the demands of my job, and I would also have the benefit of Bob's superior calling ability and know-how over mine. As daylight became more pronounced, we could clearly see the bird crouched on the limb, and each time Bob called the Tom would gobble loudly. He was about 175 yards away, and the tree towered over a large cornfield which the turk would obviously fly into upon descending from the roost.

We were ensconced in a deep ditch which provided perfect cover along with our well-camouflaged clothing. While calling and observing the gobbler, Bob explained to me the necessity of waiting until the bird came to within 35 yards of us before shooting. He predicted the turkey would fly down within 15 or 20 minutes, and since no hens were in evidence he would begin to make his way toward us and would go into full strut about 75 yards out and would slowly continue to approach us in response to restrained and selective calling. I again assured him that I understood what to expect and what I was supposed to do. I was to do the shooting while he did the calling.

Well, events unfolded exactly as Bob had anticipated and at about 75 yards out the bird went into full strut, and he was huge! He looked even bigger than the 26-3/4-pound gobbler I had shot several years earlier with my big Ithaca 10-gauge at between 45 and 50 yards. A year later I also laid low a 19-1/2-pounder at 55 yards with the same gun, although my brother-in-law, Virgil Tagtmeyer, a truly outstanding turkey hunter, who was with me at the time, had said, "Don, if you shoot one that far away again when you're with me, I'll kick you in the rear end really hard!"

So, as the enormous turk approached us in that cornfield I had been adequately warned. As the gobbler got another 10 yards closer, the bigger and bigger he looked. After another 10 to 12 yards of advancement, I told Bob that I believed he was close enough to kill. Bob said, "Are you absolutely sure,?" And I said, "Yes, I am certain that I can waylay him." Since he was deep down in the ditch and couldn't see the bird, he gave me the green light to shoot if I thought it was close enough.

The Big Ten roared and I fully expected to see the giant gobbler crumple. Instead, it jumped straight up in the air six full feet and then flew away. I threw some more lead at him as he departed toward the heavy timber across the creek. Bob jumped up as soon as I shot, and his face became livid. He snarled, "For God's sake, Dad, that bird was 60 yards away, you fool, what the h— is wrong with you?" He then picked up his things, reminding me of all the time and trouble he had gone to in scouting the bird and then calling him in the next morning, and he further said, "From now on you hunt turkeys by yourself and maybe you'll learn how to kill them properly."

Well, I was flabbergasted and deeply hurt, although I realized that he was absolutely right in every respect. We were well concealed in the set-up we had and the bird was continuing to approach us with no hesitation. There was no reason to shoot prematurely under such circumstances since, if the bird did vacillate and start to run away it could always be shot at the closer range, if only allowed to get closer in its original approach. During our long and silent walk out of the field to Bob's Suburban, I even shed some tears while thinking of my faux paux, plus missing a huge turk which would have made a fantastic mount.

After Bob's display of justifiable disgust, I figured I wouldn't hear from him the remainder of the two-week turkey season, but two days later he called me and said that he had spotted some more turks 25 miles southeast of Sedalia and there were at least three gobblers among them.

We arrived on the scene at a half-hour before daylight and set up on the edge of a large cornfield next to a creek. A long wait ensued with no sounds and no action. Finally, at 9 a.m., two gobblers came out on the field 150 yards away. We had a decoy out and we had cut some limbs which we stuck in the ground for a small blind. After 20 minutes one of the birds went back into the woods, but the other one responded to our call and saw the decoy we had set out earlier. It began to move toward us cautiously in response to calling.

I didn't move a muscle and almost ceased breathing. As the bird got within 50 yards in full strut, Bob whispered to me, "Dad, I'll tell you when to shoot." After what had occurred two days before, I protested not one iota. As the bird reached only 30 yards away, I wondered, "For heaven's sake, why doesn't he let me fire?" Another five yards closer and I really began to tense up since I was afraid the bird would spot us and pull off one of those lightning-like head ducks that turks are notorious for and then they take off in high gear and are exceedingly difficult to hit. In fact, an alarmed turk can run much faster than a jack rabbit.

At last, at 20 yards, Bob whispered, "Take him, Dad," and the bird collapsed completely when I pulled the trigger. When I picked it up, the 19-pounder with a nine-and-a-half-inch beard was like a limp rag. I felt much better, as did Bob, than two days before when the really big boy got away.

Since these two episodes, I have restrained myself concerning the longer shots, and the last nine turkeys I have bagged have all been taken at less than 40 yards, most of them at 30 or even less in some instances. I no longer have the Big Ten gauge Ithaca, having sold it to Bob, and I now have a much lighter 12-gauge Benelli which shoots three-and-a-half-inch shells.

Another thing which is crucially important to remember when going for turks is to have the gun up and ready to shoot before the gobbler presents itself, a thing I learned the hard way several years ago when two gobblers came up within thirty yards and I had seen them coming through the brush at forty yards and sat there like a dunce thinking I could easily nail one of them by raising my gun quickly after it came into full view. The bird saw me and like a flash did his "head duck" maneuver and my shot found only thin air. Since turks can both see and hear seven times better than a human they must be hunted with more skill than almost any other living thing.

THE GOBBLING, GOBBLING, GOBBLING GOBBLER!

Don Lamm, 1994

IN APRIL OF 1994, I had gotten a nice gobbler the first week of the turkey season, but wanted to bag a second one during the second week. My son, Bob, was in the same situation. We both had hunted hard, both separately and together for six days that second week but had drawn blanks.

The night before the last day of that spring season, Bob told me he had been working a large gobbler for several days intermittently about 30 miles south of Sedalia, Missouri, our home town, but he couldn't get it in close enough for a decent shot. When turkey hunting, any shot taken more than 40 yards away from the bird is highly questionable because the shot gun pellets lose much of their killing power for a gobbler's large size, and the shot pattern is not concentrated enough to be effective. A wounded bird, even when rolled over at close range, can get back up on its feet and be hell bound for freedom in the blink of one's eye, as any hunter will testify. Bob said that working together, we might be able to out-fox the evasive gobbler and deposit him in our freezer.

The next morning we were out early and tried to coax up a bird on a farm other than the one the wily turkey frequented, but with no luck. So, 9:30 a.m. found us on the property where he was lord and master. The terrain where we were included a number of sizeable cedar trees and medium-sized oak, and on the ground were patches of switch grass and low weeds. A small creek ran down into a patch of woods down on our right. Bob believed that we should sneak up closer to where he thought the gobbler might be than he had done several times earlier in the week, where he had set up too far away. We carefully did so, and Bob then set out a decoy in an open spot and told me to submerge myself in a big cedar tree just 18 yards away.

He then walked over to my right about 45 yards and sat down in front of one of the few large oak trees and began calling. The idea was that if the turk came to his call, he would get the shot. If it spotted the decoy before going to him, the bird would likely be drawn to it and I would be able to pummel him.

After three or four calls over a period of several minutes, the turkey finally gobbled about 125 yards away. Five minutes of absolute silence. Bob then gave a yelp again on his box call and the

Connie Lamm, wife of the co-author, shares a moment with her husband as they hold the 21-1/2-pound "gobbling, gobbling, gobbling gobbler." The photo was taken on the balcony of Don and Connie's suburban Sedalia home.

bird gobbled twice, this time a few yards closer. A long interval of silence again, and then Bob emitted a different call with a gadget which had proved its worth many times in the past. The turk gobbled again. Three minutes elapsed and the gobbler gobbled again without Bob's calling. He was now about 75 yards distant.

Several minutes went by in complete silence, and Bob purred softly on his call, and the bird gobbled two or three times and then kept gobbling and gobbling, one after the other. Of course, I had my gun up expecting him to show up at the decoy at any moment. But such was not yet to be. When the turk was 60 yards away, Bob was calling with great discretion and the bird was drumming and was also gobbling its head off, but because of the nature of the terrain with its cedar trees, neither Bob nor I could see it.

Every time Bob cautiously and softly clucked, now with long intervals of silence in between, the turkey would drum and gobble, moving in closer each time. In all my years of gobbler hunting, I had never heard a gobbler gobble so incredibly loud and often. The suspense was immense as I waited for him to present himself at the decoy or to hear the blast of Bob's big Ithaca 10-gauge bringing him down.

Finally, after another five minutes of absolute silence, the bird appeared like a ghost right in front of me at the decoy, in full strut, facing me. I leveled off on his head with my Benelli 12-gauge, which was chambered with a three-and-a-half-inch turkey load, and pulled the trigger. The bird collapsed completely into a heap by the decoy and scarcely even kicked.

So, Mr. gobbling, gobbling, gobbling gobbler had finally met his match! I can state with all honesty that he had gobbled at least 125 times from the time he started until he presented himself at my decoy! When Bob and I took it to the check in station, instead of weighing 24 or 25 pounds as Bob had anticipated, having seen it at a distance a couple of times earlier in the week, it topped out at 21-1/2 pounds, but its incredible gobbling performance and its full 10-inch beard more than made up for its lack of heavy weight.

Often when one can't, by himself, get a gobbler to come in close enough for a good shot, teaming up with another hunter will get the results one is seeking. It encompasses the timeless adage that two heads are better than one, and that's what is sometimes needed to out-maneuver a stubborn gobbler.

Art Lamm, Don's older son, shows off his 22-pound gobbler with an 11-inch beard which he downed in late April 2000, near Florence, Missouri.

Don Lamm, left, was proud of his 16-pound jake, but his brother-in-law, Virgil Tagtmeyer, topped him on a spring day in 1994 with his 23-1/2-pounder. Note the large, bushy beard on Virgil's bird.

Don's younger son, Bob, displays the 1-3/4-inch spurs of a 21-1/2 gobbler he took just a quarter mile from his father's home in April 2000. The turk had an 11-inch beard.

FAVORITE SHOTGUNS

Richard Cooper

Everyone who considers himself or herself a bird hunter, quail or pheasants, has a favorite shotgun and a favorite type of shotgun. Nothing which I say is going to change that preference one iota. Therefore, the following several lines represent my personal choices and no one else's, save those whom I choose to quote.

Most of you who are reading this hunt pheasants with a 12-gauge and so do virtually all the persons you hunt with. That's your choice, and I respect it. So do nearly all of my hunting companions use 12-gauges with only two exceptions which I can recall over the years. Both of the exceptions are relatives. One is my older son, Jay, who shoulders an Ithaca/SKB XL900 semi-automatic in 20-gauge. With a three-inch shell, it's a deadly weapon which will cut deeply into the numbers of all ringnecks that come within range. By the way, that range is somewhat greater than most 12-gauge carriers believe.

The other person among my hunting companions who favored the 20-gauge was my princely father-in-law, Mel Shearburn. Mel never really had an opportunity to hunt pheasants, but when he was after bobwhites, it was an endangered bird which flushed in front of him. It's a gross understatement to say that he was deadly with his little Browning A5 20-gauge.

I started pheasant hunting in 1959, the year I graduated from Kansas State University. Like nearly everyone else, I believed that the only size shotgun to use was 12-gauge. It was not until several years later when I was hunting quail in Kansas with my wife's 20-gauge Remington 58 that I came to realize that a 20 was quite adequate. The pheasants were almost non-existent that year, but the quail population was quite high. Frank Russell and I had made a trip to check it out, and we were not disappointed. Each of us had

141

no trouble in filling out his limit of eight birds both days, usually within two hours. On the second day, a rare ringneck jumped up in front of me, and I scored a clean kill with a 2-3/4-inch shell loaded with 7-1/2s. I became a devotee of the 20-gauge from that time forward.

At the end of a tiring day's hunt, a 20-gauge is a much more comfortable gun to be carrying. For me, at least, a 12-gauge is more like carrying a cannon, and it makes my arms ache. However, there is a price to be paid for carrying a lightweight 20-gauge loaded with high base shells, and that is recoil. If you're recoil sensitive, you may not want to try it. However, if you get so caught up in the excitement of the hunt, as I do, that you don't notice recoil, then a 20-gauge may just be the ticket. I never notice recoil during a day's hunt until I see a strange purple area developing on my right shoulder the next day.

My personal choice for pheasants is a Franchi semi-automatic in 20-gauge. At just five and one-half pounds, it handles like a wand. It has only a 2-3/4-inch chamber, but I have found baby magnums in 20-gauge to be more than adequate. It also holds five shells which can be an invaluable feature on certain rare occasions. Check the regulations of the state where you're hunting first. Some, such as Missouri, require a shotgun to be limited to three shots, even for upland game. My personal second choice for pheasants is an Ithaca/SKB Model 900 semi-automatic in 20-gauge. It weighs only a half-pound more than a Franchi and has the advantage of a three-inch chamber. This long recoil shotgun hasn't been manufactured for many years and was replaced by the XL900 which was gas operated. Although none of these shotguns is currently in production, there are still a fair number of them around. I am unable to say if any newer versions of them are on the current market.

For quail, I find the side-by-side double to be the epitome of grace and balance. Single or double triggers are a matter of choice. My personal choice would be a 20-gauge double with a single selective trigger bored improved and modified. With today's screw-in choke tube feature on even double barrels, a wide variety of chokes is available.

Several years ago, the case was made so memorably for the side-by-side 20-gauge double by the late Jack O'Connor, one of America's greatest outdoor writers and a lover of the sleek little gun. He wrote, "The 20-gauge double barrel is among shotguns what a well-stacked blond is among women."

I have made no mention of the over-and-under, or stack barrel. Many hunters love them, and there are many excellent ones on the market. However, if you intend to purchase a good one, or a good side-by-side for that matter, be prepared to pay a price in four figures.

A BASS FISHING BONANZA
AND BUNNIES GALORE

Don Lamm, 1941

DURING MY TEENAGE YEARS, which encompassed most of the 1940s, one of my closest friends came to be Jim Kahrs, who I discovered enjoyed the out-of-doors as much as I. One day in freshman algebra class we commenced conversing about fishing, and I told him I never had experienced the opportunity to catch any really nice bass and that I really didn't know anything about it.

He immediately asked me if I was doing anything the coming weekend and I replied no. He then said, "Then we'll ride our bicycles down to Uncle Art Eicholtz's place on Lake Creek and I'll show you what bass fishing is all about." The time was early November, and when we arrived at our destination by mid-afternoon, which was 16 miles southeast of Sedalia, Missouri, the creek was crystal clear and we unloaded our fishing poles by a deep hole of water where a big tree had fallen in some years before.

The next task was to get some bait with which to catch some fish. I hauled out my big coffee can, the top of which had some holes in it, and said, "Well, Jim, I'm all ready to go looking for some big grasshoppers; I'm sure glad it's a warm day." He then remarked, "Grasshoppers, my foot, Don, we're going to seine some big minnows, grab one of those minnow buckets and the seine." I did as he told and 20 minutes later we were standing at our fishing stations, Jim on one side of the sunken tree and me on the other, each with a bucket full of nice-sized chub and shiner minnows.

Jim then set his bobber so that the bait would sink down into the water five or six feet, and I did likewise. This was after he had first hooked a minnow through the back. I followed suit, but I really didn't think we were going to get anything doing all of this because my mind set was still riveted on grasshoppers as the "only" bait to use. But, WOW, what a surprise I got when I saw Jim's bobber suddenly disappear rapidly under the surface of the water, meaning that something big had grabbed that minnow and was headed for its lair. Jim skillfully allowed the fish time to swallow the bait and then he heaved it up on the bank, a four-pound big mouth black bass.

Three minutes later the identical thing happened to me, and I was rewarded with a three-and-a-half pounder. To make a long story short, by late that afternoon we both had our stringers loaded with our limit in bass plus several large blue gills and a couple of channel cats. Jim's aunt and uncle were both delighted when we brought our catch in, and they helped us clean it. Needless to say, we all thoroughly enjoyed our bountiful and tasty fish supper and more fish at noon the next day before we got back on our bicycles and rode back to Sedalia.

One other adventure I had, among many with Jim, which stands out markedly occurred a couple of years later when we were both 16 years of age and juniors in high school. I told him I had just gotten a neat Christmas gift from my father, a 22 long rifle Winchester pump which held 14 shells, and that I had been practicing with it and had even hit quite a few rabbits on the run.

He then remarked, "Well, my mother gave me a cool four-ten gauge shotgun and I've gotten good with it, too." I then said, "Jim, I'll bet you five dollars that I can hit more cottontails on the run with my rifle down at Lake Creek in one full day's hunting than you can score on with your four-ten." He said, "You're on, and you'll lose."

That Saturday we were down at Jim's uncle's farm, and we also had permission to hunt on some neighbors. In fact, they all showed keen interest in our bet. During the day we walked and walked, and over all we jumped at least 40 rabbits, and our cottontail shooting tally see-sawed back and forth all day long, first Jim in the lead and then me. Jim was indeed quite shocked at how effective I was with that 22, and I must confess that I was quite surprised myself. It finally got close to dark and we were tied at seven and seven, with both of us yearning for just one more shot before we could no longer see. Finally, a bunny jumped up just at dark in front of Jim and, BOOM, he rolled it and I walked back with him to his Uncle Art Eicholtz's house five dollars poorer!

Today, Jim is the owner of Osage Fish Hatcheries at Osage Beach, Missouri, and his wife, Liz, and their three sons are very active in the enterprise, and they have done exceedingly well. I occasionally see him, and our boyhood days at Lake Creek and out on my father and uncle's farm always come up in the conversation.

Lessons to be learned from this account are to have an open mind about new ways to catch fish and not to get over-confident about how well you can shoot a new firearm, especially when money is involved.

MY FIRST THRILLS OF FLY FISHING

Don Lamm, 1941

WHEN I WAS about 15 years old, I never had caught a fish fly fishing. I had caught bass, large perch and a few catfish with a pole and bobber using grasshoppers and minnows as described in another story in this book entitled, "A Bass Fishing Bonanza and Bunnies Galore."

My next door neighbor, Mr. Lee H. Peabody, Sr., of Sedalia, Missouri, was the father of one of my closest friends who was my same age. Mr. Peabody was an enthusiastic fly fisherman and a superb catcher of frogs, and many a time I had seen him come back home after an outing loaded with two stringers of fish and at least 10 or 12 frogs. I had always watched with interest as he dressed them, and at times he gave me some fish and frogs for my mother to fry for a delicious dinner for our family.

One Saturday afternoon he asked me to go fishing with him and his wife, who liked to fish with pole and bobber while sitting up on the creek bank using grasshoppers and minnows as bait. Mr. Peabody asked me to help him seine some minnows for his wife to use for catching bass, since their son, Lee Jr., did not feel well and could not go. Mr. Peabody also said he'd loan me a fly fishing rig and some flies and show me how to fly fish. I was elated at the opportunity to go with him.

We traveled about 10 miles south of Sedalia, and Mr. Peabody then drove to Doc Hausam's cabin which was on Spring Fork Creek, a crystal clear stream which had been one of the principal sources of fish and frogs for Mr. Peabody for years. Doc Hausam, my dentist during my early years, was as good a fisherman and frog catcher as Mr. Peabody.

Upon arrival at the doctor's cabin, Mr. Peabody lined me up to help him seine some minnows, and then he fixed me up with the proper fishing equipment and showed me how to use it. He gave me several flies which included underwater spinners, bucktails and surface poppers, and he indicated that recently he had been having good luck with bucktails, which are bushy-haired underwater lures. He attached one to my line and gave me some special tips on what to expect when a fish struck.

Upon getting into the creek, he had us split up and he sent me one way and he went the other. He emphasized that he wouldn't return until about dark, which was about two hours hence, and when he did he would then spend some time hunting some bullfrogs with a strong flashlight.

Not expecting to do well due to my inexperience, one can imagine my surprise when I felt a jerk on my line by a sizable fish, but I missed setting the hook properly, and a nice large mouth bass got away. Three minutes later, however, the same thing happened and I was ready. It was a real thrill playing that fish on that tackle, and a few minutes later I had a two-and-a half-pound large mouth bass on my stringer.

Continuing on up the creek I hit some good holes of water with weeds and other excellent cover along the bank, and not only did I catch several more bass weighing between a pound and two pounds and a quarter, but I caught some large hand-sized perch as well.

Upon joining Mr. Peabody at near dark, he looked at my fish and congratulated me on a job well done, for I had caught almost as many as he, and my one largest bass had topped his biggest one. He then proceeded to frog hunt for an hour or so and returned with nine large hoppers which he said would make delicious eating this coming weekend, and both his wife and my mother were really good cooks.

So, that's how I got initiated into fly fishing! Of course, having caught those bass and big perch with Jim Kahrs down at Lake Creek the year before as described in detail in my story in this book entitled, "A Bass Fishing Bonanza and Bunnies Galore," I decided I wanted to try fly fishing Lake Creek by myself.

Early one Saturday morning found me ready to fish what was soon to become one of my favorite stretches of water on the creek. My money belt was loaded with large popping bugs, bucktails and other varieties of flies, and I had two fish stringers and a knife strapped around my waist. Since I didn't cater to waders in my teenage years, I had on a bathing suit and tennis shoes. The water was cold as I stepped into it at 7 a.m., even though it was the second day of June, and I shivered for a while, but after beginning to move downstream and catching three or four nice perch in the process, I warmed up considerably.

Then I approached a hole close to a half-mile long, which we called the "Cabin Hole," because Jim Kahrs and I, plus a few other select friends, had stayed in a cabin owned by a relative of Jim's which was located on a timbered ridge above the creek and had experienced a number of pleasant weekends there. So that stretch of water below the cabin came to be labeled that name. At various times I had observed that the hole had some nice fish.

As I slowly and cautiously moved into the hole, I soon had a sharp strike on a big bucktail, and a two-pound large mouth black bass gave me some exciting rod play. Putting him on one of the stringers, I glowed with satisfaction that I had such a nice bass to take home. I then picked up two sizable blue gills which fought on the line with a lot of scrap.

Then, looking up ahead in the creek about 60 yards, I noticed the flop of what appeared to be a large fish at the top of the water about a foot or so out from the left bank. I said to myself, "Aha, this must be a really good bass, and I must get him on my line and into the skillet." I substituted a big black popping bug for the bucktail lure and approached the place carefully where I had seen the fish break water just moments before and flipped out the lure, causing it to light softly at exactly the place intended.

The fish shot up into the air a foot and a half on the vicious strike, and I knew I had him hooked solid! I played him cautiously for about five minutes so as to wear him out before bringing him closer so he wouldn't break the line, break loose the hook or snag up on a tree root. During the time I was playing him, he broke the surface of the water with one or two more jumps and circled around me twice.

The large mouth black bass weighed slightly over three and a half pounds, which wasn't bad for a creek bass and, at the age of 15, it was the largest fish I had caught up to that time and I was very proud of it. My father, who always took great interest in my hunting and fishing activities, paid to have the fish mounted, which didn't cost a great deal in the mid 1940s. Today, the expense of mounting a fish of any size at all is quite steep. As of today, the fall of the year

2000, I still have that bass mount on the kitchen wall of our home.

For over 30 years after the above described episode, I fly fished Lake Creek and two other creeks near Sedalia at least once every two or three weeks, sometimes more often. Of course, this was undertaken from mid-May to the end of September; then the weather got too cold and the hunting season had started, especially on doves. For the past 23 years I haven't been down there to Lake Creek to fish, only to occasionally hunt turkeys, but the memories of that creek and the wonderful times it gave me will never be forgotten. I introduced both of my sons to fishing on that creek and they, too, think of it with great fondness.

My now 43-year-old son, Bob, who hunts turkeys in the Lake Creek area, told me that the old cabin where I used to stay with Jim Kahrs on the bluff above the old fishing hole where I caught that three and a half pound bass 58 years ago is still there, only in a completely run-down, dilapidated state — now just a faint icon of yesterday's America.

CARL JOE, THE INQUISITIVE CROW

Don Lamm, 1942

NEARLY EVERY YOUNG PERSON loves pets, and in my midteens during the early 1940s I often hunted crows on my cousin Beasmore Lamm's father's farm just west of Smithton, Missouri. Bease and I would go out into the woods with a crow call and try to coax these highly intelligent and keen-eyed birds within shotgun range, but most of the time we came up with blanks.

One morning about ten o'clock while we were standing among a group of large shag bark hickories, I looked up and observed a rather large bird nest with some relatively small black objects sticking their heads over the edge of it. I asked Bease what kind of birds they might be, and he said, "Don, they are very young crows, and here's your chance to get yourself another unusual pet." By that statement he meant that the summer before he had helped me catch several snakes, some of which I had taken home with me.

I shinnied up the tree, peered into the nest and plucked the biggest of the four out of its lair and brought it to the ground. For the next several months I raised Carl Joe on milk, boiled eggs and oatmeal. He grew and grew and bonded with me completely, seldom leaving me entirely alone.

Shortly after he began to grow into maturity, I realized that he needed a suitable name, and I selected the name of Carl Joe in honor of Carl Romig, the great foreman for many years on my father and uncle's 1100-acre farm just west of Sedalia, Missouri, and Joe Mulkey, a black, who was a good-natured, intelligent, friendly, hard-working hired hand.

After Carl Joe grew up, I would take him out to the farm, and he would ride on the tractor with me, perched on my shoulder. Seldom did he try to associate with the wild crows, somehow knowing that he was different. He collected all sorts of shiny objects and deposited them in little piles in the garage and garden at my parents' home in the town of Sedalia.

Other birds in the neighborhood pestered Carl Joe unmercifully, especially the blue jays, and I deplored this, but there was little I could do about it. Carl Joe would sometimes alight upon the head and shoulders of my mother and father as well as upon mine, and they endured it with no protest. Indeed, during my childhood I was very lucky to have such loving and understanding parents.

One fine mid October day, a very elderly lady was walking down the sidewalk in front of our house. She had a large amount of grey hair on her head, and I saw that Carl Joe, who was perched on a limb in a sugar maple, was intrigued. All of a sudden he crouched down on his perch and then launched himself from it, sailing down until he reached the very top of that woman's head. Of course, the dear lady was completely taken aback, not realizing at all what was happening to her, and she started screaming loudly, grabbing at her hair and running down the street as fast as she could. Carl Joe then flew up in the air, just as frightened as she, and came back to me for assurance. When I finally caught up with the lady to explain to her what had happened and why, she showed a lot of hostility which caused me not to sleep well that night. I never did see the woman walk by our house again even after Carl Joe died.

In fact, some weeks after the above-described incident, I found Carl Joe at the base of a large elm tree in our yard, dead. We never knew whether someone had poisoned him because they were annoyed at all of the noise other birds emitted when they pestered him, or because that old lady or her kin contrived to do him in, or because the other birds ganged up on him and pecked him to death. Anyway, I was very sad about it all and buried him in the garden with his precious treasures.

Many hunters and farmers consider crows to be a nuisance, and they do their best to kill as many as they can either by poison or by gun whenever they have the time, and in my youth I also attempted to thin their ranks via firearm.

A number of years ago I ran into Beasmore, and we began talking about our earlier years of crow hunting, Carl Joe and snake catching. I had long since ceased hunting crows due to lack of time, plus having more tasty birds to pursue such as doves, quail, pheasants and waterfowl. I then asked him if he still hunted crows and he said, "No." I asked him why and he told me that one day when he was in one of his fields he saw several crows a quarter of a mile away down on the ground running around. He related that he glassed them carefully with binoculars and, lo and behold, they were catching field mice and eating them. "That," he emphasized, "convinced me that they did much more good than harm and I'll never try to kill one again."

One could also make the same argument for non-poisonous snakes which kill thousands and thousands of insects, mice, rats and other small animal pests each year that do damage to grain and property, plus spread disease. People who gleefully run over snakes with their cars while they are crossing the road or kill them with rocks or other contrivances are grossly misinformed, and they need to educate themselves concerning the value of non-poisonous snakes in the world of nature, and they also need to learn which snakes are poisonous and non-poisonous. The wanton killing of thousands of rattlesnakes each year for commercial exploitation is indeed one of the saddest scenarios in America.

OUTDONE ON DOVES BY MY WIFE'S GUN

Don Lamm, 1979

SHORTLY AFTER my wife, Connie, and I got married 23 years ago, she told me one September afternoon that she wanted to go dove hunting with me. Up until that time I had not been aware that she was interested in such an activity, in fact, I didn't even know that she knew how to shoot a gun!

I told her, "Honey, it's mid-September and it's hot outside; I don't think you're up to it. We'd better go together some other time when it's cooler." She replied, "I'm no sissy, Donald, and I can stand the heat just as well as you."

Well, that did it, and 4 p.m. found us out in a farmer's cornfield starting to look for doves. When I dove hunt, I prefer walking to sitting, even in hot weather, because one gets a good many jump shots which hones his or her shooting prowess for quail, pheasants and ducks later on in the year. Connie also wanted to walk and do likewise, but I emphasized that it was too hot for her to walk the distances that I intended to go and that she needed to go over by that big dead tree and sit or stand under it. I also thought that her chances of killing some birds were much better there because they'd coast in slowly as they reached the tree and she'd also perhaps get the benefit of some doves I might flush up and miss which might fly her way. I also surmised that, at best, she would get three while I limited out at 10.

As the hunt progressed, I did a considerable amount of shooting after walking quite some distance from each direction of the tree. I also heard Connie shooting a lot, and I said to myself, "My God, she is wasting a lot of shells and I bet she's hardly getting any!"

Sometime later, being worn out from walking, with six birds in the bag, I started back to the tree. I hadn't heard Connie shoot for the past 20 minutes, so I figured she had run out of shells and had wasted most of them. What a surprise it was when I saw her with 10 doves all lined out as I approached. Unthinkingly, I remarked, "Did you get all of those by yourself or did someone help you?" She coolly replied, "Of course, I got all of them by myself, you ninny, did you ever see anyone under this tree with me? How many birds did you get?" I told her, and then asked, "Who in heaven's name taught you how to shoot so well?" She stated, "A teacher of mine, my dear old daddy, got me started, but after that I taught myself."

Many men fail to realize that their wives and daughters would like to learn to shoot and to hunt if only they were introduced to it gradually and without undue kidding or criticism. Trap and skeet shooting pay big dividends here, as well as brief hunts during good weather. In modern America today, more and more women are becoming involved in hunting, fishing and outdoor activities of all kinds, and that will help keep them more healthy both physically and psychologically.

NOT ABOUT HUNTING (OR, THE CASE OF THE NERVOUS CALF AND THE BIG BLACK BUICK)

Richard Cooper, early '70s

IT WAS A COLD January morning in the early 1970s, and the forecast called for scattered areas of freezing rain, sleet, or snow. For my long-time hunting companion, Bill Glenn, it was an especially busy morning, what with an eight o'clock dental appointment and a favor for a neighbor to be completed before opening his loan and investment office at nine o'clock.

Everything was thoroughly laid out so that all bases could be touched unless something occurred which could upset his clockwork plan. Enter Murphy's Law!

Bill lived about seven miles northeast of Sedalia and farmed part-time raising cattle. A neighbor purchased one of his large calves each year to refill his freezer with beef, and this was the morning to deliver the calf to Pettis County Locker for slaughtering and processing. Bill had installed the stock rack in his pickup the evening before in preparation for the delivery.

The next morning was extremely cold, but there was not a trace of the unwanted precipitation. He completed his chores, loaded the calf and ate a quick breakfast before changing clothing in preparation for the trip into town. Before completing half of the journey, it began to sleet, and the highway showed signs that it had been sleeting from there into town for quite some time. Consequently, his intended speed of 45 miles per hour was reduced to no more than 15, and he arrived in town just in time for the dental appointment. The calf would have to be delivered after the dental appointment, not exactly what Bill had planned.

He pulled into the dentist's empty parking lot with the calf getting more nervous by the moment. By this time, the sleet had stopped, and it was getting noticeably colder.

During the 30 minutes in which he was getting a fresh filling, someone in a shiny, black Buick parked in the space next to his calf-laden truck. When he returned, Bill was not prepared for what he encountered. The increasingly nervous calf had spewed last night's rations out through the space between the bars of the stock rack and onto the passenger's side of the Buick's windshield. Being so cold, the molten mess flowed only partway down the side of the car before it froze.

As the calf stomped and snorted, Bill debated what to do. To the best of his knowledge, he had never seen the Buick before, and it was already after 8:30 with a stop still to be made at Pettis County Locker. He finally confided to himself, "To hell with it," and headed out to deliver his by then highly odorous cargo.

Now, nearly 30 years later, Bill says he still has no idea whose car got so offensively decorated. "Maybe the owner no longer lives in Sedalia, or maybe he's even dead. However, if he's still in the area, I may get killed the day after this book is published."

EPILOGUE

No BOOK ON HUNTING would be complete without a few words on ethics, not only as far as abiding by the law is concerned, but also as it applies to personal conduct and relationships.

If you have a son or daughter, possibly a grandson or grand-daughter, approaching the age of 10 or 11, a careful and responsible introduction to the sport of hunting is a good thing. This should be preceded by a season or two of accompanying you as a walking companion before allowing the carrying of a gun.

Above all, teach care and caution in all gun handling. Treat all guns with the utmost respect. Assume that all are loaded. NO EX-CEPTIONS! Gun safety training is not only required by law in most states for those born in the late 1960s or later, it is something which all of us should be subjected to no matter what our ages.

Respect the game which is being hunted. Hunting seasons only allow the harvesting of a reproductive surplus. Do your part in protecting the resource so that there will be a harvestable surplus for hunters in future years. Remember, daily and possession limits are not objectives always to be achieved; they only place restrictions on potential game hogs. Far more important is being immersed in the great outdoors, getting an occasional shot, and enjoying the camaraderie of good friends.

Respect the landowners on whose property you hunt. After all, they hold the key for most of us in determining hunting success or failure. Always secure their absolute permission and know the boundaries of the property. Remember, you are only a guest; always be a courteous one. Leave the property the way you found it. If you open a gate, close it after you; if it is already open, leave it open. Let the landowner know you appreciate him, and show this by cultivating a year 'round relationship. If the opportunity presents itself, do some favors for him. A few minutes getting a stray cow back into a pasture or picking up thoughtlessly thrown litter will pay dividends far greater than the hunting time lost. At Christmastime, remember him and his family with a card and a sincere note of good cheer.

Never, never drink a drop of alcoholic beverage while hunting. Reserve that for the end of the day, and place strict limits on it even then.

With this approach, hunting should always be an enjoyable experience. Have a great time, and keep your powder dry.